URBAN TRAILS

RENO

URBAN TRAILS
RENO

Galena · North Valleys
Washoe Valley · City Parks

HELENA GUGLIELMINO

MOUNTAINEERS BOOKS

MOUNTAINEERS BOOKS is dedicated to the exploration, preservation, and enjoyment of outdoor and wilderness areas.

1001 SW Klickitat Way, Suite 201, Seattle, WA 98134
800-553-4453, www.mountaineersbooks.org

Printed in China
First edition, 2025

Design: Mountaineers Books
Layout: Chloé Dorgan
Cartographer: Lohnes+Wright
All photographs by the author unless credited otherwise
Cover photograph: *Wedekind Regional Park (Trail 9)*
Frontispiece: *Looking west on the Truckee River from Wingfield Park (Trail 2)*
Leave No Trace Seven Principles © Leave No Trace, www.LNT.org

Library of Congress Cataloging-in-Publication data is on file for this title at https://lccn.loc.gov/2025011054.

Printed on FSC-certified materials

FSC www.fsc.org MIX Paper | Supporting responsible forestry FSC® C188448

ISBN (paperback): 978-1-68051-746-0
ISBN (ebook): 978-1-68051-747-7

An independent nonprofit publisher since 1960

CONTENTS

NORTHWEST RENO

SOUTHWEST RENO

SPARKS AND SOUTHEAST RENO

GALENA

WASHOE VALLEY

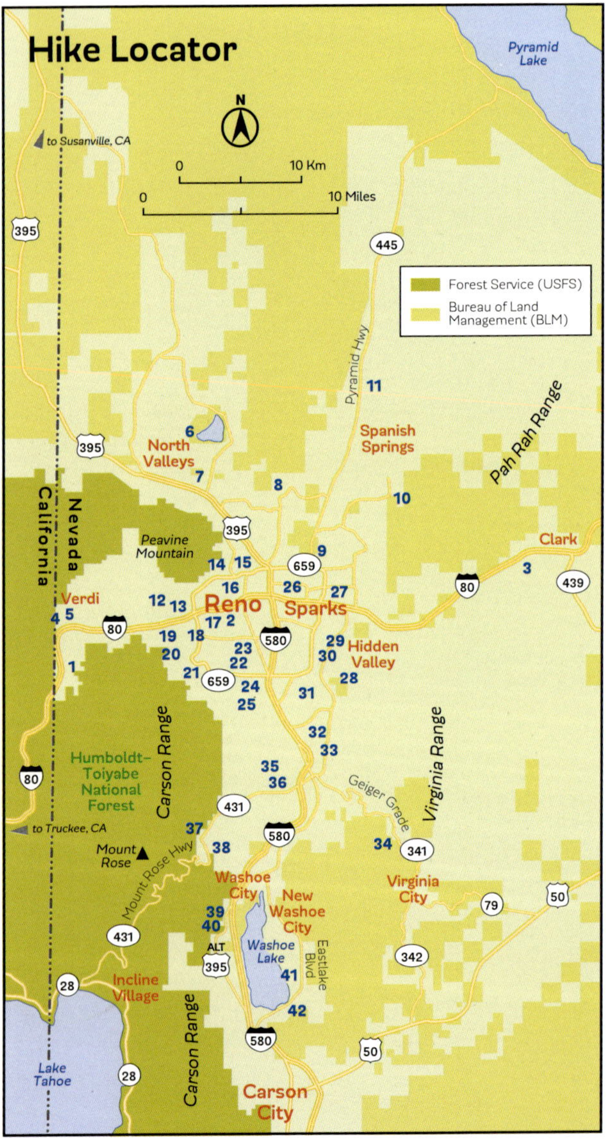

Hike Locator
N
0
10 Km
0
10 Miles
Forest Service (USFS)
Bureau of Land Management (BLM)
Pyramid Lake
to Susanville, CA
Pyramid Hwy
Pah Rah Range
Spanish Springs
North Valleys
California
Nevada
Peavine Mountain
Clark
Verdi
Reno
Sparks
Hidden Valley
Humboldt-Toiyabe National Forest
Carson Range
Virginia Range
Geiger Grade
to Truckee, CA
Mount Rose
Mount Rose Hwy
Washoe City
New Washoe City
Virginia City
Washoe Lake
Eastlake Blvd
Incline Village
Lake Tahoe
Carson City

TRAILS AT A GLANCE

Trail/Park	Distance	Walk	Hike	Run	Bike	Kids	Dogs
TAHOE-PYRAMID TRAIL							
1. Verdi to Fleish Bridge	7.2 miles	•	•	•	•	•	•
2. Idlewild to Wingfield Park	3.5 miles	•		•	•	•	•
3. McCarran Ranch Preserve	4.2 miles	•	•	•	•	•	•
VERDI							
4. Crystal Peak Park Interpretive Trail	0.5 mile	•				•	•
5. Verdi Nature Trails	0.5 mile	•				•	•
NORTH PEAVINE AND PAH RAH							
6. Swan Lake Nature Study Area Trail	4.4 miles	•				•	
7. North Valleys Regional Park	2.4 miles	•	•	•	•	•	•
8. Sun Valley Regional Park	2.1 miles	•	•	•	•	•	•
9. Wedekind Regional Park	3.3 miles	•	•	•	•	•	•
10. Sparks Regional Trail System	4.2 miles	•		•	•	•	•
11. Sugarloaf Peak	5.5 miles	•	•	•		•	•

Trail/Park	Distance	Walk	Hike	Run	Bike	Kids	Dogs
NORTHWEST RENO							
12. Sierra Vista Park	1.8 miles	•	•	•	•	•	•
13. Rainbow Ridge to Las Brisas	4.3 miles	•		•	•	•	•
14. East Keystone Canyon Loop	4.4 miles	•	•	•	•	•	•
15. Evans and Vista Loop	4.1 miles	•	•	•	•	•	•
16. Rancho San Rafael Regional Park	3.2 miles	•	•	•	•	•	•
SOUTHWEST RENO							
17. Oxbow Nature Study Area	0.9 mile	•				•	
18. Caughlin Ranch Path	5.4 miles	•		•	•	•	•
19. Tom Cooke Loop	3.8 miles	•	•	•	•	•	•
20. Hunter Creek Falls Trail	6.2 miles	•	•	•		•	•
21. Cold Canyon Loop	3.8 miles	•	•	•	•	•	•
22. Steamboat Ditch Trail	3.1 miles	•		•	•	•	•
23. Virginia Lake Loop	1 mile	•		•		•	•
24. Bartley Ranch Regional Park	2.1 miles	•	•	•	•	•	•
25. Ballardini Ranch Loop	2.2 miles	•	•	•	•	•	•
SPARKS AND SOUTHEAST RENO							
26. Teglia's Paradise Park	1 mile	•		•	•	•	•
27. Sparks Marina Park	2 miles	•		•	•	•	•

Trail/Park	Distance	Walk	Hike	Run	Bike	Kids	Dogs
28. Highland Loop	2.6 miles	•	•	•	•	•	•
29. Rosewood Nature Study Area	2.5 miles	•				•	
30. Erica Greif Memorial Bikeway	11.9 miles	•		•	•	•	•
31. Huffaker Hills Loop	3 miles	•	•	•	•	•	•
32. South Meadows Neighborhood Paths	3.9 miles	•		•		•	•
33. Damonte Ranch Park	3.3 miles	•		•	•	•	•
34. Toll Road Trail	5.6 miles	•	•	•	•		•
GALENA							
35. Lower Thomas Creek Trail	5.7 miles	•	•	•	•	•	•
36. Lower Whites Creek Trail	7.2 miles	•	•	•	•	•	•
37. Church's Pond	6.6 miles	•	•	•		•	•
38. Brown's Creek Trail	5.2 miles	•	•	•	•	•	•
WASHOE VALLEY							
39. Davis Creek Park	2.1 miles	•	•	•	•	•	•
40. Ophir Creek Trail	4.4 miles	•	•	•	•	•	•
41. Dune Trek	5.6 miles	•	•				•
42. Deadman's Creek Trail	1.2 miles	•	•	•		•	•

LAND ACKNOWLEDGMENT

THE TRAILS IN THIS BOOK are located at the western edge of the Great Basin. The Waší·šiw (Washoe) were the first inhabitants of the immediate land where Reno and Washoe Valley is today, with a legacy dating back thousands of years. The Numa or Numu (Northern Paiute) territory overlaps the Washoe's and extends north through what is now Spanish Springs and into Pyramid Lake (and beyond). Other tribes like the Newe (Shoshone) and the Nuwuvi (Southern Paiute) were close neighbors in southern or eastern parts of the Great Basin.

These tribes had great wisdom and traditions closely tied to the land, from pine nut harvesting to basket weaving, that live on today in vibrant communities. We are grateful for all that these communities, rich in history, have to teach us.

Opposite: *Aspens in spring along Lower Whites Creek Trail (Trail 36)*

Next page: *A stormy sunset above Slide Mountain and Washoe Lake, as seen from the Dune Trek (Trail 41)*

INTRODUCTION

GETTING TO KNOW RENO

LOCAL WRITER AND SELF-DESCRIBED ECOCRITIC Michael Branch once endearingly described Northern Nevada as an alien place that "looks like it wants to kill you all the time." He shared this observation with me in an interview three years after I reluctantly moved to Reno. The environment made me uncomfortable—so open, so dry, so close to defining the fragility of life. The closest suitable nature, I mistakenly thought, was somewhere in the Lake Tahoe Basin.

With time pressing on each day, trips to Tahoe became less accessible. I needed a natural outlet closer to home. On one of my first local hikes, a journey on the southeastern flank of Peavine Mountain, I felt feverish in my rush over loose rocks to find some sort of silence, some sort of solitude. I craved the still calm of nature wrapping its arms around me, but the low brush did little to quell this. As I climbed higher and higher up the hill, past the landmark N at Rancho San Rafael Regional Park (Trails 15–16), my resentment grew. Finally, I came to the top of the mountain and sat, delirious with want and frustration, on an outcrop of pointy red rock. I grumbled toward the wind, as if my anger could stop it from pushing hair into my eyes. As I sat there, I vowed to move to Oregon or Montana—someplace characterized by pine and water.

The Truckee River near Tom Cooke Trail (Trail 19) and Mayberry Park

After realizing the futility of reasoning with weather, I looked up to Mount Rose and across the cup of development to the Virginia Range. Clouds with seams of golden sunlight cast a glow over the scene that made me pause. After a few deep breaths, I noticed the kaleidoscope of reds, browns, oranges, and pinks of the rock supporting me. The light, dusty sage in the foreground, a contrast that played against the colors of the rock. Each element of nature built upon itself right in front of my eyes.

The wind blew the clouds into a different orientation and the landscape changed again. New canyons within the mountain ranges stood forward, new folds across the hillsides revealed themselves. Like the darting of a common fence lizard, the sight felt impossible to hold onto, impossible to keep. The landscape around me demanded my attention; moments spent elsewhere—looking at my phone, picking up my camera, turning to wrangle my dog—felt comparatively insignificant.

As I walked back to the trailhead, my neighborhood in sight, I felt incredibly lucky and proud to live in such a place. All these years later, I pity the people who ask with judgment, "You still live in . . . *Reno*?"

Michael Branch advocates for this land through his writing, exposing the possibilities that are often overlooked in favor of softer places. "The sheer vastness and starkness of this place attracted me and then worked on me slowly, over time, like wind on a rock, until I had no ambition greater than to make a life in these high, dry wilds," he wrote in *Rants from the Hill*. I hope the book you now hold in your hands provides a similar inspiration to explore the hillsides and peaks that, from a distant first glance, seem monotonous, exposed, and dreary.

This guidebook details forty-two trails, both natural and paved, within neighborhoods and extending into the open space surrounding the urban areas. I have intentionally excluded trails in the Lake Tahoe Basin, showcasing instead the beauty and variety of Northern Nevada's high desert. If you find that a hike along Peavine doesn't suit you, don't be discouraged. Try another trail, a different time of day, or a different time of year. Explore when clouds are cast over the Sierra. Explore in time to see the sunset. Slow down and seek native wildflowers or migrating birds. There is not a single trail in this book I wouldn't happily return to, and many beyond the bounds of these pages to explore.

GEOGRAPHY

Reno and a good portion of Sparks sit within the Truckee Meadows. The Carson Range towers over the western horizon; the Virginia Range over the eastern. Peavine Mountain, crowned with radio towers, is a prominent fixture to the north of town. The geologic history of the area is complex, with many overlapping events. This area has a lot of volcanic and hydrothermal activity, was submerged underwater at some point, and is continually changing from tectonic forces that pull the state apart. It sits on the western edge of the Great Basin and is characterized by a generally arid landscape, sagebrush, and the endless views of mountain ranges. Because the Sierra Nevada are so close, water does find its way to the Truckee Meadows, and wetland habitat, streams, and riparian areas are abundant south of Peavine and west of the Virginia Range. The hikes in this book explore each environment the area has to offer, as well as some prominent geologic features. Look for sidebars that dive into deeper details about the local features and geography.

The Truckee Meadows, North Valleys, and Washoe Valley have so many trails, it's hard to narrow down the very best to share here. Even though I thought I knew them, initially proposing a list of more than seventy trails to my editor, there were still surprises. In writing this, I found new places I had no interest in before—or had overlooked. A couple of them—Sun Valley and the Toll Road—I wouldn't have hiked had I not had an assignment to write about them. There are hidden gems everywhere, and though you may have favorites, don't let your routine stop you from exploring more.

WEATHER

Surprising to few, Reno has about three hundred days of sunshine. Though a common perception is that Reno's weather is similar to Las Vegas's, it's actually cooler here. Summer

Hiking among the pines on Ophir Creek Trail (Trail 40)

temperatures hover around 95 degrees, and at least a few days of snow should be expected in the winter. The biggest weather, however, is wind. The average speed of local wind is 6 miles per hour, though gusts of more than 80 miles per hour have been recorded. Wind happens year-round. Prepare for it when hiking; bring a hat, tie your hair back, and take deep breaths of patience. Though Reno sits within the rain shadow of the Sierra, dramatic clouds still make their way over the ridgeline. These are some of the best days to hike, as dramatic shadows reveal new perspectives on the surrounding mountains.

The glow of sunset in the eastern sky, as seen from the trail to Church's Pond (Trail 37)

WHAT TO PACK

Most routes in this book are not extensively time consuming or far from urban settings. While this may inspire casual packing, always carry the Ten Essentials. The point of the Ten Essentials, originated by the Mountaineers, has always been to answer two basic questions: Can you prevent emergencies and respond positively should one occur (items 1–5)? And can you safely spend a night—or more—outside (items 6–10)? Use this list as a guide and tailor it to the needs of your outing.

1. **Navigation.** Always carry a map of the area you are hiking in and a compass, and know how to use them. Offline maps are available through various apps.
2. **Illumination.** Bring a headlamp and spare batteries, in case you get stuck outside in the dark.
3. **Sun protection.** Wear a hat or head covering, sunglasses, and sunscreen rated at least SPF 30. Lightweight long-sleeved sun shirts are a great way to keep shoulders and arms covered and protected.
4. **First aid.** There are lightweight first-aid kits for hiking that you can grab at any outdoor store. For casual hikes, this might include bandages, pain relievers, blister treatment supplies, antiseptic, ointment, a compression wrap for sprains, anti-inflammatory tablets for swelling, and antihistamine tablets for emergency allergic reactions (like bee stings!). If you've been prescribed an inhaler or EpiPen, bring it with you.
5. **Repair kit.** Bring a knife or multitool, duct tape, and other supplies in case you need to repair gear, such as your backpack.
6. **Fire.** Carry waterproof matches or a lighter, and firestarter, in case you get caught outside overnight.
7. **Shelter.** Take a lightweight bivy sack, emergency blanket, or large plastic trash bag.
8. **Nutrition.** Always bring snacks, and pack more food than you think you'll need. Hiking burns a lot of calories and you may be hungrier than normal, even if you don't realize it.
9. **Hydration.** Carry enough water. Also consider bringing a water filtration system or tablets if there is water along the trail.
10. **Insulation.** Dress in layers and bring extra clothes. It is almost always windy in Reno, and when your shirt is sweated through at the top of a hike, wind can cause discomfort or unsafe body temperatures.

WILDLIFE SAFETY

Many animals call the high desert home, including bears, mountain lions, coyotes, rattlesnakes, and horses. Though sightings and interactions are rare, it is important to understand what to do when faced with one of these animals. Please also note that feeding any wild animal (even chipmunks) is not okay. Wild animals should be kept wild, even in urban areas, as dependence on human food can negatively affect their behavior.

The best way to avoid an animal interaction is to make noise and announce your presence on the trail. Sing a song if you hike alone, or engage in a round of twenty questions when hiking with others. If you see a dead animal that has been gnawed on, leave the area immediately—likely there is a territorial predator coming back to its feast.

BEARS

Black bears are not a common sight in the Sierra foothills, though sometimes they travel to lower elevations. If you encounter a black bear while hiking or visiting open space, keep children and dogs close, slowly back away while facing the animal, and make noise (like saying "hey bear"). Change your route to give the bear an escape route and to avoid making the animal feel trapped.

Do not run. Do not act aggressively. Stand your ground and do what you can to look large (like waving trekking poles in the air) if a bear approaches you. If attacked, fight back. Bears can be seen any time of day.

CATS

Mountain lions (also known as cougars or pumas) and bobcats both roam the area. Most likely you will never see one. If you do, follow precautions similar to those you would for a bear encounter. It is especially important to not run away from a cat—that response ignites its prey drive. If things turn sour, throw whatever you can at the cat, avoiding crouching

Along the Highland Loop (Trail 28), a lizard suns itself on a rock with Reno in the background.

down or making yourself smaller. Fight back if attacked. Cats are most likely to be seen during dawn and dusk.

RATTLESNAKES

In our hot, dry environment, rattlesnakes should be expected everywhere. The Great Basin rattlesnake is known by herpetologists as one of the least aggressive and shyer species of rattlesnake. However, do not ever underestimate the defense of a snake. Do not ever try to pick up, handle, or kill a rattlesnake if you find one on the trail.

Your pet is the most at risk of a snake bite. Dogs love to stick their nose in sagebrush, romp around, chase bunnies, and approach unknown entities face-first. All of these actions put rattlesnakes in defense mode. By keeping your pet on a

The male California quail's signature comma-shaped crest serves as a distinct marker for this common bird.

leash, you will protect it from a snake encounter. Rattlesnake avoidance training is very popular as well; it teaches your pet to have a negative association with the sight, smells, and sounds of a snake.

If you or your dog are bitten, try to do the following: take a picture to identify the snake in question, keep your (or your pet's) heart rate as low as possible, elevate the bitten area if possible, remove any constricting items (rings, watches, collars, etc.), and seek help immediately. Most hospitals and emergency vets keep antivenom available, but it is best to call ahead to confirm and to inform doctors of the situation so they can act as quickly as possible. Do not ever apply a tourniquet, suck the blood out, or ice the wound.

Like most wildlife here, the Great Basin rattlesnake does not want to interact with humans. It will do everything in its power to get out of your way. If you see a snake on the trail, give it room and let it move itself to safety. If it begins rattling, back up and give it space. Rattlesnakes should be expected when temperatures are between the high 60s and mid-80s; if you are comfortable in a T-shirt, expect snakes to be active.

WILD HORSES

Wild horses roam the Virginia Range on the eastern side of Reno. Do not ever approach or feed a wild horse, as their temperament is unpredictable. You will likely see them when hiking in this area. Give them space, changing routes when necessary to avoid them. Learn more about Nevada's wild horses by reading the sidebar near Highland Loop (Trail 28).

SHOOTING AND FIREARMS

The state of Nevada has the highest amount of federal land (at 80.1 percent!), and with this land of many uses comes territory for shooting. Near some trails, like Sugarloaf Peak (Trail 11) and Sparks Regional Trail System (Trail 10), you may hear gunfire. To see where shooting is and isn't allowed, visit the Washoe County Firearms Discharge Restrictions Map (see Bureau of Land Management in Resources).

OUTDOOR ETHICS

The basic tenet of outdoor ethics is to leave the area better than you found it. As users of the outdoors, it is our responsibility to care for the local environment. An easy way to ensure this is by following the seven fundamental Leave No Trace (LNT) principles:

1. **Plan ahead and prepare.** This means researching weather, the route you plan on hiking, and packing the right gear.
2. **Travel (and camp) on durable surfaces.** The best way to ensure this is to stay on trail when hiking in wild places. Other acceptable surfaces include rock, gravel, dry grasses, and snow.
3. **Dispose of waste properly.** Often there are no trash cans available on trail. Pack out all trash (including dog waste) and throw it away in an appropriate container.

4. **Leave what you find.** During spring especially, when wildflowers are aplenty, it is tempting to take a piece of nature home. But if everyone did, we'd have nothing to wonder at, and wildlife, insects, and other plants can suffer.
5. **Minimize campfire impacts.** Do not start fires while hiking, and if you must while camping, make sure current conditions permit it.
6. **Respect wildlife** . . . and they will respect you. Refer to Wildlife Safety above if you need to review specifics.
7. **Be considerate of others.** Hopefully this guideline needs no explanation.

Beyond these principles, consider the effects of social trails, which we have a lot of locally. Created by hikers and cyclists, these trails have not undergone permitting and environmental impact studies and do not take into consideration historical or cultural sites. Traveling on these trails may be unsafe and can lead to erosion and loss of habitat for flora and fauna. Though it can sometimes be difficult to distinguish social trails, try your best to stay on designated routes. The best ways are to follow the directions in this book or look at official trail maps from Washoe County, City of Reno, Truckee Meadows Trails, and others.

Another thing to consider is the many ways people recreate on our local trails. Hiking, cycling, horseback riding, shooting, birding, off-roading—our public land is used by many. Please be respectful of all trail users. Yield to uphill traffic, move off-trail for OHV (off-highway vehicle) users, and communicate clearly.

VOLUNTEER FOR TRAILS

The trails need our help! While there are a staggering number in the area, they do not maintain themselves, and most of the work is up to volunteers. A number of organizations, like the ones listed below, and local businesses, like the Gear Hut, offer ways to get involved. From clean-ups to breaking trail,

A happy pup enjoys the views from Sugarloaf Peak (Trail 11).

here are some local organizations that need your help (see Resources for contact information).

- Tahoe-Pyramid Trail
- Keep Truckee Meadows Beautiful
- Biggest Little Trail Stewardship
- Truckee Meadows Parks Foundation
- Friends of Nevada Wilderness

If you've made it through reading this entire introduction, first of all congratulations, and second of all, please don't be overwhelmed. Nature is beautiful but cares nothing for your safety. You have to empower yourself to navigate and arrive prepared. My advice is to start small, choose a hike that is close to home (I'm sure there is at least one in this book!). Bring a loved one along with you, or at least let someone know where you're going and when you expect to be home. Tackle a couple of miles for your first trip, then add more. You'll get the hang of it.

Next page: *Along the trails in Bartley Ranch Park (Trail 24), a wooden structure covers Last Chance Ditch to keep the waterway clear of rocks.*

HOW TO USE THIS GUIDE

THIS GUIDE IS FOR THE PERSON who just moved to Reno, just as much as it is for the longtime local. The trails described are aimed at providing an experience for everyone. They range from 0.5-mile loops to 18-mile point-to-point trails, and from 20 feet of elevation gain to 2400. But don't just step onto the trails that match your perceived experience and fitness level; challenge yourself to walk the paths that seem below and above you. Although I am a thru hiker and lover of big climbs, one of my favorite nature explorations is the half-mile boardwalk at Swan Lake (Trail 6).

Hiking in the high desert lends itself to possibility, its wide-open landscapes begging an expedition. This guide is intended to spark your curiosity about the area and give an introduction that leaves room for personal discovery.

I've walked each of these trails to curate a list that represents the area's varied environments. My experiences are backed up with information from the Truckee Meadows Trails' databases, knowledge from the program coordinator for the Washoe County's Trails Program, and the experiences of daily users today and throughout history. Still, the trails in this book change with the occurrences of heavy winters, continued development, social trails, and unforeseen happenings.

Please be sure to do your research (Leave No Trace principle 1) and understand current trail conditions and maps.

This book details forty-two routes, both paved and natural. Paved routes are referred to as "path," while routes traversing natural ground are referred to as "trail."

KEY TRAIL INFORMATION

Each trail description begins with a block of key information containing the following:

Distance. This category provides the length of the trail in miles. Each distance indicator also notes the type of trail: loop, out-and-back, and point-to-point. Loop and out-and-back trails both start and end at the given trailhead; point-to-point hikes indicate the mileage and route from a starting trailhead to an ending access. Point-to-point routes only occur for trail systems that span more than 10 miles, such as the Steamboat Ditch Trail (Trail 22). Distances were calculated using CalTopo GPS from my hikes and cross-referenced against other data sources. However, they may vary slightly.

Elevation gain. This number is a cumulative overview of the elevation gained (rounded to the nearest 10 feet), again calculated from my hikes and cross-referenced with local data. There might be slight differences in these numbers, but generally, they will be a guide to what to expect. Elevation gain is one metric of difficulty (see below), but generally, a slope less than 400 feet per mile is easy, 400–600 is moderate, and 700–1000 is challenging. Most loop and roundtrip routes in this book resemble an upside-down V, meaning the uphill sections mainly occur only one way. Church's Pond (Trail 37) is a very challenging hike, gaining almost 700 feet per mile, but the bright side is that it's all downhill on the way back!

High point. This line indicates the highest elevation of a trail, rounded off to the nearest 10 feet, unless the high point is a clear, officially measured summit or point. Generally, on loops or roundtrip routes, this will be the midway point, but

Views east from where the Cold Canyon Loop (Trail 21) meets Hunter Lake Road

not always. The high point is not an indication of weather, as this environment sits within the rain shadow of the Sierra Nevada and can be fickle.

Difficulty. Rating a trail's difficulty is as subjective as personal interpretations of modern art. What may be easy for you may be difficult for someone else. The rating accounts for an average adult ability and ranges from easy to challenging. The rating considers a trail's elevation gain, length, surface tread, and navigation. If a trail is marked as "Moderate" or "Difficult," there will be a brief explanation within the trail introduction describing why.

Fitness. This notes the best use of the route, such as walking, hiking, running, or cycling. Trails usually note suitability based on tread and elevation gain. Relatively flat or paved routes are labeled good for walkers, runners, and cyclists, while more strenuous elevation profiles on natural tread are relegated to hikers. But if you feel the need to run to Church's Pond (Trail 37), don't let the fitness category stop you.

Cyclists must yield to hikers, keep their speed under control, and be able to stop or adjust at a moment's notice.

Views from the bench at the top of the Fisticuffs section of East Keystone Canyon Loop (Trail 14)

Downhill traffic yields to uphill traffic. Please announce yourself to other trail users and slow speeds around corners and blind switchbacks.

Family-friendly. Because parents know their children's ability best, I use this section to note the ADA accessibility, stroller suitability, and any special cautions to be aware of, such as cliffs, uneven terrain, and so on.

Dog-friendly. Most trails are dog friendly; however, a few—like Oxbow Nature Study Area (Trail 17)—are not, due to sensitive habitats. Washoe County requires that dogs be on a leash no longer than 6 feet, with the only exceptions being Wedekind Regional Park (Trail 9) and Mount Rose Wilderness (Trails 20 and 37). Even when permitted to be off-leash, dogs must be under complete voice control at all times, but note that keeping dogs on-leash during the warmer months can help protect them from encountering a rattlesnake (see the Rattlesnake section above, page 23, for more information).

Please pick up after your dog. Though local wildlife poops in the environment, a domesticated dog's waste is not natural to the surroundings. We feed our pets processed foods and give them medications, vaccines, and supplements; our pets' excrement carries traces of this. Our dogs are also confined to a single route when we use local trails, resulting in piles of poop and ruining the experience of a trail. Keep Truckee Meadows Beautiful cited as much as 80 pounds of poop gathered at Huffaker Hills during one trash cleanup day. In some areas, there may not be trash cans beyond the trailhead, so be prepared to carry poop bags along the trail.

Amenities. Amenities can include picnic areas, drinking water, restrooms, playgrounds, pet waste stations (pet waste bags and trash cans), and more. Restrooms and drinking water may be available only during the warmer months; those with year-round availability will be noted. When traveling in open space (land outside of urban areas or parks), practice the following Leave No Trace principles: do your business (number 1 and 2) at least 200 feet from the trail and from water, bury solid waste in catholes 6–8 inches deep, and pack out toilet paper and hygiene products..

Contact. This category notes the land manager or managing organization in charge of maintaining the route. Our area has dozens of managers, and some trails have more than one. In this book, the most relevant agency is noted. Websites and contact information can be found in the Resources section at the back of this book. Many of these managers also provide printable maps (or maps you can save to your phone) on their websites, which is noted when applicable.

Several trails are public-use trails within homeowners association (HOA) properties, which will be noted in this section. For these types of trails, it is important to respect all private property and follow all posted signs.

GPS coordinates. Here you will find the coordinates of the trailhead (WGS 84) in decimal degrees, listed with north

Looking through the trees at the southern end of the pond in Davis Creek Park (Trail 39)

value first and west second with a minus symbol. While many of these routes are located at well-known places that most mapping apps recognize, some, like the Verdi to Fleish Bridge section of the Tahoe-Pyramid Trail (Trail 1) are a bit harder to find. Enter a trail's GPS coordinates into your mapping system to get the precise location and best driving directions.

Before you go. This section highlights important information, like park hours and special considerations, for each route.

DRIVING DIRECTIONS AND TRAIL DESCRIPTION

These sections highlight unique features of the trail and provide directions to the trailhead. Turn-by-turn directions will help you find your way, while notable landmarks and flora are called out.

Getting there. Public transit options, if available, are provided in this section, most often with the Regional Transportation Commission (RTC) of Washoe County; learn more at rtcwashoe.com. Turn-by-turn driving directions are provided from major interstates, highways, and local roads.

Trail overview. A brief overview of each trail lets you know what to expect. It includes details about scenery, location, points of interest, history, and wildlife.

Map. Each trail includes a map focused on the featured route, including select options such as the Go Farther routes.

Get moving. This section contains turn-by-turn trail directions, as well as interpretive information and perhaps a personal story or two. It may also include a turnaround point for a shorter option for those who want to hike only part of the trail. The map will also have information to help you find your way and notice points of interest.

Go farther. This section includes a variety of options, depending on a given trail and possible connections, such as a turnaround point for a shorter option for those who want to hike only part of the trail.

Next page: *A Roezl's penstemon along Cold Canyon Trail (Trail 21) with downtown Reno in the background*

GUIDE TO COMMON NATIVE FLORA

Though from far away the mountainsides of Nevada look similar, they are alive with variance. From the springtime wildflowers to the very rocks that make up the mountains, each hike in this book can reveal a new secret of Nevada. The next few pages features photos of the area's common flora, the plants I reference most throughout this guide—though you will certainly encounter many more species while exploring. Wildflowers can be found year-round in this region, but most species bloom between April and early July.

COMMON NATIVE WILDFLOWERS

1. Apricot mallow
2. Arrowleaf balsamroot
3. Beckwith's violet
4. Bighead clover
5. California poppy
6. Lupine
7. Mariposa lily
8. Mule ear
9. Paintbrush
10. Phlox
11. Prickly poppy
12. Twinleaf onion

COMMON NATIVE TREES AND SHRUBS

1. Antelope bitterbrush
2. Curl leaf mountain mahogany
3. Desert peach
4. Dorr's sage
5. Fremont cottonwood
6. Great Basin sagebrush
7. Hopsage
8. Jeffrey pine
9. Quaking aspen
10. Rubber rabbitbrush
11. Singleleaf pinyon
12. Utah juniper

TAHOE-PYRAMID TRAIL

Though various pedestrian and motorized routes have historically followed the Truckee River, modern access to its waters has been limited or locked behind private land. Seeking to correct this issue, local cycling enthusiast Janet Phillips founded the Tahoe-Pyramid Trail in 2003, which strung together 114 miles of trail along the Truckee River, from its origin at Lake Tahoe to its terminus at Pyramid Lake.

Besides its overwhelming beauty, the endearing quality of this trail is Phillips herself. People called her "a dynamo" and appreciated her creative approach, like riding a bike on Interstate 80 to demonstrate the need for a bike path connecting Reno and Verdi. Close encounters with trucks convinced enough people, and the trail broke ground in 2004. Phillips thought it would take only five years to build, but it has been nearly twenty-one. Only two sections east of Sparks are left to add.

Through Phillips's vision and enduring passion, the Tahoe-Pyramid Trail provides access for walkers, hikers, trail runners, cyclists, birders, photographers, and anglers. The organization hopes that, once completed, the trail will also serve commuters between Reno and USA Parkway's business complex, lessening I-80 traffic and local emissions. While the trail provides increased recreation opportunities and celebrates the Truckee River, the reason it headlines this book is its power to connect communities to the nature around them.

Opposite: *A mountain biker enjoys shade from Fremont cottonwoods in the McCarran Ranch Preserve section (Trail 3) of the Tahoe-Pyramid Trail.*

1 Verdi to Fleish Bridge

DISTANCE: 7.2 miles roundtrip
ELEVATION GAIN: 570 feet
HIGH POINT: 5330 feet
DIFFICULTY: Moderate
FITNESS: Walkers, hikers, runners, cyclists
FAMILY-FRIENDLY: Yes
DOG-FRIENDLY: Yes, leashed
AMENITIES: None
CONTACT: Tahoe-Pyramid Trail, download map from website
GPS: 39.486608°, -119.9920411°
BEFORE YOU GO: Sections intersect private property; follow posted signs. Periodic trail closures along Truckee Meadows Water Authority property; visit TPT website for details.

GETTING THERE

Driving: From I-80 west, take exit 3 for Verdi. Turn left off the freeway onto South Verdi Road. Continue for 0.2 mile onto Crystal Park Road, then take the first left onto Quilici Ranch Road. Continue for 1.6 miles along the dirt until it dead-ends. Park on the right.

A walk west along the Truckee River is an adventure that never stops. From Verdi clear into Truckee, California, the trail allows users to keep venturing around the next bend with curiosity.

Reno residents can put the city behind them without driving more than ten minutes on the freeway. This new landscape, pointed westward into the alluring Truckee Canyon and sided by the peaks of Mount Rose Wilderness, contrasts starkly with what many of us see in our daily urban lives. Not only that, this section is quiet and less frequently visited than places like Peavine Mountain (Trails 14 and 15).

As you prepare for this trail, be aware that bears, mountain lions, and other wild animals have been sighted in the

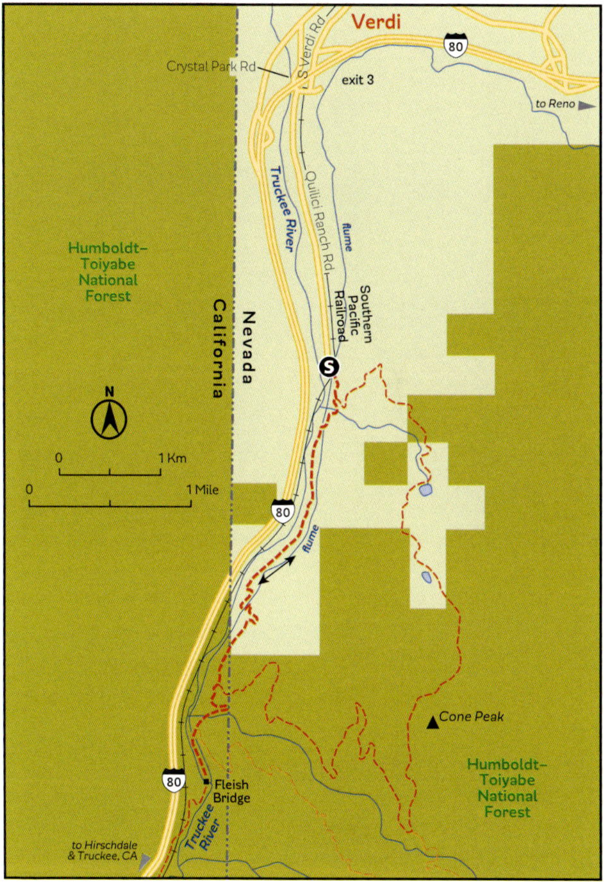

area. Also, sections cross railroad tracks and approach near Interstate 80; supervise children.

GET MOVING

From the trailhead parking lot, look south across the train tracks for the cheerful blue Tahoe-Pyramid (TPT) sign that

Fleish Bridge over the Truckee River

guides you along the trail. Cross the tracks with caution and meet the dirt trail, which begins with an immediate uphill push.

At 0.2 mile, ignore the Forest Service road that spurs left (south) from the trail. In late spring and summer, watch for a trove of wildflowers along this section, including purple Lewis flax, phlox, and desert peach.

The trail winds along the hillside, over a lovely stream, to the start of land managed by the Truckee Meadows Water Authority (TMWA). Here, at the 0.4-mile mark, trail users must duck or walk around an access road gate. Follow the TPT signs, which clearly mark the path. Dogs must be leashed in this area—no exceptions. The trail takes you straight west from the gate, shortly arriving at a TPT kiosk with a map and historical information. Read the TMWA informational placard before you enter this shared space. Remember that access to trails crossing private property is a privilege—not a right.

About 250 feet from the gate, the trail curves right (north) toward the river. Here, the Fleish power plant comes into view, along with a train trestle crossing the river. Follow the TPT sign, which directs users to the left (west). Along this stretch, notice a waterfall shooting out from a flume. While artificial, it is beautiful as it spills into a small pond surrounded by greenery. The trail here is easy to follow, marked on the south side with fencing. At 0.6 mile, cross a pedestrian bridge and continue westward.

Though you are now out of the main TWMA area, several access roads intersect the TPT as the trail heads west. Each is clearly marked with both No Trespassing signs and TPT markers. The trail levels with the Truckee River again, though access is prohibited to allow for healthy riparian growth and protect habitat for many native species.

At 0.8 mile, look up and left (south) to see the wooden structure of an old box flume that supplied water for hydroelectric power plants (like the historic Farad plant; see Go Farther for directions). Virginia City mines demanded a lot of power, and hydroelectric was a great option to replace coal and wood. The mining town received its first jolt of power from the Truckee River in 1900. Farad's power plant closed in 1987, but TMWA still uses hydroelectric plants like Fleish.

Around 0.9 mile, river access opens up. This spot is very popular with fly fishers, though the fast-moving river can be very cold and speckled with invisible boulders, especially in spring or after significant storms.

At 1.3 miles, the trail enters a forest of incense cedar and Jeffrey and ponderosa pine, offering much-appreciated shade. The ponderosa and Jeffrey are very similar; they both excrete that vanilla-butterscotch smell and have deeply fissured bark. The cones are the real way to tell them apart; generally, ponderosa cones have scale points that face out, while Jeffrey's point down. "Prickly ponderosa, gentle Jeffrey" is a way to remember it. You may also start to notice wildflowers like silvery lupine and balsam arrowroot. This forested area offers the classic Sierra Nevada experience: dry trail, large and well-spaced trees, low underbrush, and filtered sunlight casting a gorgeous glow.

At 1.8 miles, the trail makes an abrupt left turn south before switching back west within 300 feet. This zigzag marks the start of a 300-foot climb over the next mile. Once the trail begins to straighten back up to the west, enjoy a lovely little waterfall from a creek as a nice reward.

The environment becomes much more open now, trading pines for giant blazing stars and Great Basin sagebrush. About 750 feet from the waterfall, the trail again turns south before crossing a stream. Gain elevation steadily while moving east, south, and then finally reverting west. At 2.1 miles, the trail returns to the forest. At 2.4 miles, a sign welcomes trail users into California.

At 2.8 miles, you immediately begin to descend. Over the next 0.4 mile, watch your footing, as the trail becomes very rocky and steep. At 3.1 miles, continue straight and then turn sharply north to cross a bridge, before walking west again along a fjord of the river.

At 3.6 miles, the trail comes to the Fleish Bridge over a large dam in the river. This suspension bridge sways and rocks with the weight of its passengers, a slight disturbance for anyone wary of the rushing water below. Cyclists must dismount to cross. On the other side, a bench makes the perfect place to sit and relax. When you're ready, reverse your route back east to Verdi.

GO FARTHER

There are many ways to extend this hike. The TPT connects all the way from Verdi to Lake Tahoe, though you must traverse along the road in spots. The best way to extend is to set up a car shuttle or arrange a pick up at either Farad or Floriston, both of which have exits on I-80. Farad involves another

5 miles and 490 feet of gain, while Floriston adds 6 miles and 560 feet. This section gets closer to the highway, but fantastic views of the Truckee and the northern edge of Mount Rose Wilderness, as well as river access and a hidden hot spring make up for it.

Another alternative is to hike to Cone Peak, either from the start or on the return. From the Verdi trailhead, turn left after 0.2 mile onto a trail that splits off to the left. Enjoy a 2500-foot climb over 4.1 miles, past Fuller Lake, to the summit. The peak is beautiful, and the quiet trail is a great way to relieve stress.

A RIVER OF HISTORY

The Truckee River (or wakhu wa't'a, as the Washoe people call it) has been part of human history for thousands of years—potentially even tens of thousands! The written history we know of starts in the nineteenth century. It is widely thought that the river (and town) gets its name from a Paiute chief who helped a scouting party of immigrants create a route from the Great Basin into the Sierra Nevada. The chief repeated "tro-kay," meaning "all right." However, immigrants mistook this saying as a personal identifier and began calling him Chief Tro-kay, which eventually changed into Truckee.

This route along the Truckee River created a way through Donner Summit, where the 1847 Donner Party events took place. For the most part, it parallels the transcontinental railroad and Lincoln Highway, both of which provided the first means of their kind to connect the East and West Coasts of the US. This new access paved the way for the 1870 train robbery, the aftermath of which led to the 1871 Carson prison break and the naming of Convict Lake near Mammoth Lakes. It also led Reno to become the Divorce Capital of the World (because of its lenient grounds for divorce). To signal they were starting a new life, divorcees would cast their wedding rings into the Truckee River in downtown.

Since the late 1800s, the Truckee has been used for commercial purposes, supporting lumber mills, breweries, agriculture, and the growing needs of Reno residents. Each section of the Tahoe-Pyramid Trail has a historical story to tell.

2 Idlewild to Wingfield Park

DISTANCE:	3.5 miles roundtrip
ELEVATION GAIN:	Up to 200 feet
HIGH POINT:	4550 feet
DIFFICULTY:	Easy
FITNESS:	Walkers, runners, cyclists (must bike on road between Idlewild and Wingfield Parks)
FAMILY-FRIENDLY:	Yes, ADA and stroller accessible
DOG-FRIENDLY:	Yes, leashed
AMENITIES:	Benches, swimming, restrooms, barbecue grills, sports fields, pet waste station, public art, picnic tables, rentable shelter
CONTACT:	Tahoe-Pyramid Trail, download map from website
GPS:	39.521841°, -119.83298°

GETTING THERE

Public Transit: The RTC 16 stops in three spots along Idlewild Drive: Booth Street, Cowan Drive, and Hunter Lake Drive. Hunter

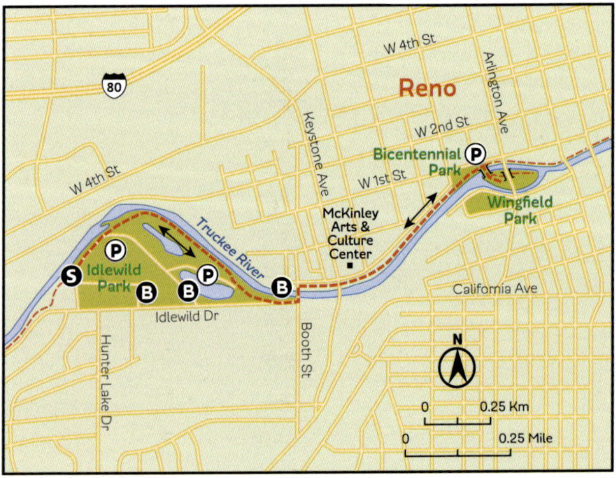

Stunning colors at Idlewild Park during fall

Lake Drive is the closet to the start of this hike; walk west 300 feet to Latimore Drive, turn right, and join the path.

Driving: From I-80, take exit 12 for Keystone Avenue. Head south for 0.6 mile. After 1st Street, stay in the right lane to access the Keystone frontage road, under the bridge. It dead-ends at Riverside Drive; turn right. Continue 0.1 mile, then turn left on Booth Street. Cross the river and turn right onto Idlewild Drive. After 0.2 mile, turn right onto Cowan Drive.

Access the main parking area by taking the first right onto Mastroianni Drive, and the second area along Cowan after it turns into Latimore Drive. In summer and sometimes during the year, there are events at Idlewild Park, McKinley Arts & Culture Center, and Wingfield Park that impact parking. Check Visit Reno Tahoe's website for details (see Resources).

Looking west along the Truckee River between Idlewild and Bicentennial Parks

This paved section of the Tahoe-Pyramid Trail (TPT) is a wonderful path along the Truckee River through one of Reno's historical neighborhoods and three notable parks: Idlewild, Bicentennial, and Wingfield. Spring through fall offer an excellent time to visit, when the brilliant cottonwoods, oaks, and willow trees are on full display. The canopy of mature trees and breezes coming off the Truckee make it feel 10 degrees cooler than anywhere else in town. It is a special place.

Public art, like the famous *Portal of Evolution* butterfly sculpture, line the trail along Bicentennial Park. Families bring their young children (and dogs) to swim in the Truckee River's pools in summer. This section is also part of the city's whitewater park, so kayakers are frequently seen here practicing technical skills. Local businesses, from coffee shops and French bistros to hair salons and gyms, surround the trail, making it an ideal place to meet friends and get outside.

GET MOVING

From the Latimore Drive parking lot at Idlewild Park, locate the trail that parallels the Truckee River. Head east and enjoy the beauty of Idlewild Park for roughly 0.6 mile. This 49-acre park includes baseball diamonds, sports fields, a skate park, a pool, play areas, and a rose garden. But perhaps the best feature is the stunning Fremont cottonwoods that tower over the riverbank. Their heart-shaped leaves capture the Nevada sun during the warmer months—especially stunning during "golden hour"—and shimmer bright gold during the fall. The trail takes you underneath these beauties, with the relaxing sounds of the river's rushing waters right below.

At 0.1 mile, the trail forks; the right path leads to the primary Mastroianni Drive parking lot. Take the left trail that hugs the river, to avoid walking over the grassy area. While it is open to recreators (and can be a nice place for a picnic), be warned of the exhausting expanse of goose droppings.

Continue along the river, watching the water surge over rocks toward its ultimate destination downstream at Pyramid Lake.

At 0.6 mile, arrive at the easternmost point of the park, marked with a change from the wide asphalt bike trail to a sidewalk. Here, continue east for less than 300 feet to Booth Street. Cross to the east side of the street, then continue over the bridge to rejoin the trail parallel to Riverside Drive.

This section is flanked by grass and a variety of stunning trees. After passing under the Keystone Bridge (at about 0.8 mile), notice the McKinley Arts & Culture Center across Riverside Drive. Charming the neighborhood since 1909, this stunning Mission Revival–style building houses art galleries and occasional workshops, as well as Feed the Camel food truck events on Wednesdays during the summer.

The trail meanders east and narrows at 1.1 miles, now bordered by flower beds instead of grass on the north side. Here, downtown's skyline comes into focus. The 0.3-mile stretch to the Wingfield Park Bridge is punctuated with public art, manicured landscaping, and beautiful river views. After crossing the bridge, arrive at Wingfield Park, which sits on a river island and is divided by Arlington Avenue. Keep to the north end of the park and cross under Arlington via a tunnel to see the rest of the park, or turn around and head back to Idlewild Park.

GO FARTHER

For more, extend this walk east or west along the TPT, as both ways include a series of riverside parks. To head west, follow the path from the Idlewild parking lot as it juts out from the park, paralleling Idlewild Drive. Though this side of the trail is sometimes along the road (including Mayberry Drive), the parks it connects to are wonderful places to explore; visit Ivan Sack Park, Crissie Caughlin Park, and Dorostkar Park before landing in Mayberry Park, about 4.6 miles from the trailhead.

To head east, set out from Wingfield Park; the trail travels an additional 8 miles through downtown Reno and Sparks.

Look for historical buildings, like the Riverside Hotel (now Wild River Grill and Sierra Arts Foundation) and the Old Post Office building. After leaving downtown, the trail winds along the river, traveling through Fisherman's Park, Gateway Park, Rock Park, Glendale Park, and Cottonwood Park on its way through Sparks.

3 McCarran Ranch Preserve

DISTANCE:	4.2 miles roundtrip
ELEVATION GAIN:	110 feet
HIGH POINT:	4300 feet
DIFFICULTY:	Easy
FITNESS:	Walkers, hikers, runners, cyclists
FAMILY-FRIENDLY:	Yes
DOG-FRIENDLY:	Yes, leashed
AMENITIES:	None
CONTACT:	Tahoe-Pyramid Trail, download map from website
GPS:	39.55103°, -119.55757°
BEFORE YOU GO:	Open dawn to dusk; obey signs and stay on trail; wild horses and reptiles commonly sighted

GETTING THERE

Driving: From I-80 east, take exit 28 toward Patrick Avenue. Continue onto Waltham Way for 0.2 mile, then veer right to stay on Waltham. After another 0.2 mile, make the first right onto Wild Horse Canyon Drive. Continue for 0.1 mile and make the first right onto a dirt road. Continue to the end and park.

Surrounded by semi-arid brown and gold hills, this section of the Tahoe-Pyramid Trail (TPT) is an unfrequented oasis. Restored wetlands and river rehabilitation brought the

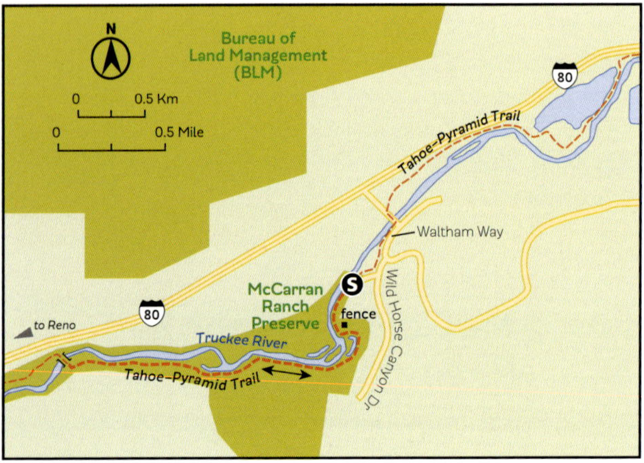

Fremont cottonwoods, tall grasses, and birdsong back to this section of river—a true contrast to the landscape around it. Even with the buzz of Interstate 80 in the distance, the trail remains quiet, shaded, and serene—worthy of the drive from Reno. Visit from early spring to late fall to see the foliage at its height, but the gorgeous Northern Nevada landscape can be appreciated any time of year.

GET MOVING

Locate the trailhead by looking for the sign at the northwest corner of the dirt parking lot. Within this section, watch for maroon-colored trail signs from The Nature Conservancy instead of the bright blue TPT signs used on other sections of this bi-state trail.

From the trailhead (one of three along this segment of the TPT), river access is almost immediate. Within 300 feet, the mixed-surface trail dips down and meets the river at a nice sandy beach. On high river years, the water is about 2 feet from the trail. If hiking during the heat of summer, this beach is a great place to dip your toes for a post-hike reward.

WETLANDS IN THE DESERT

Wetlands serve as a transition zone between bodies of water and land. In Nevada, this could be seasonally dry areas like playas and ephemeral washes, as well as springs, meadows, and riparian areas. Although swampy, shallow waters might produce a nose-wrinkling smell and parties of bugs, wetlands serve incredibly important functions. They capture carbon dioxide, act as a filtration system for pollutants in the environment, and prevent flooding and erosion. Many species also call wetlands home, including several listed as threatened or endangered.

When non-Indigenous people began to settle the area, they dammed, canaled, and irrigated the Truckee River to develop agriculture, mining operations, and residential areas. To prevent flooding, the river was also straightened out and widened in places. The Nature Conservancy (TNC) estimates that these actions caused the loss of about 90 percent of the adjacent riparian forest and 70 percent of dependent bird species. The manipulation of the Truckee River also threatened Lahontan cutthroat trout and the endemic Cui-ui fish.

Since 2003, TNC has worked to restore McCarran Ranch Preserve by naturalizing the shape of the river, recreating destroyed rapids, replicating habitat to encourage the return of native species, and replanting lost cottonwoods. Because of this work, there has been a 17 percent increase in vegetation, as well as wetland restoration in this section. While representatives at TNC say the area has not returned to its preindustrial habitat, the area has improved greatly.

In about 300 feet, the trail becomes rocky. Large, buried rocks and small loose ones cover the trail for the next 0.1 mile, potentially forcing bikers off their saddle, as the trail continues south. Though this section might not be the most pleasant underfoot, be sure to keep an eye out for beautiful wildflowers like apricot mallow during spring and summer. Look through the Guide to Common Native Flora at the beginning of the book to familiarize yourself with blooms like this one.

The trail comes to a fence at 0.2 mile as the rocks lessen their grip on the trail. This next section features smooth dirt

Looking east over the Truckee River

underfoot and a "forest" of tall, beautiful sagebrush. It transforms again as the trail curves, the brush forest giving way to the first of many wetlands. Within the first half mile, this trail has already revealed many different environments, another reason this section is so magical.

Most of this trail is under the cottonwoods, a good sign of The Nature Conservancy's work to restore the wetland habitat. A sign notes more about the restoration process, if you'd like to learn more. During spring and summer, the canopy of cottonwoods creates welcome shade, a reprieve from the heat. Be sure to take your time through here to appreciate hidden wildflowers and the calls of birds.

The trail gives peeks of the river here and there before gaining about 25 feet and coming through the trees. At 1.8 miles, it reaches a plateau above the river with a superb view, then dead-ends in another 0.2 mile. Turn right here, heading north toward the river. In 190 feet, reach a bridge, which marks the end of this section.

Enjoy views to the west of Mount Rose, then return the way you came. As you head back, be mindful of the sharp left turn you'll have to make to get back onto the trail. The sign is a bit hidden behind some greenery.

GO FARTHER

This section of the TPT extends 2.9 miles to the west and 4.9 miles to the east, occasionally hopping on roads to supplement the natural path. To go farther west, cross the bridge at 2.1 miles, then continue along the trail, with Mount Rose and Slide Mountain in the distance. The section unceremoniously ends in Mustang, where you will retrace your route back to the trailhead.

For those wanting to extend a bike ride, head east from the trailhead. This section features a lot of wide trail with big open scenery.

Next page: *The Verdi Nature Trails (Trail 5) are a great dog and kid-friendly stroll.*

VERDI

Situated in the Sierra Nevada foothills, the unincorporated town of Verdi is named after the Italian composer, Giuseppe Verdi. When he had to name the town, Charles Crocker, founder of the Central Pacific Railroad, pulled Verdi's name from a hat and proclaimed it so.

Born with the railroad and situated in the pines, Verdi's lumber trade blossomed. The mills here helped build Virginia City as the local gold rush brought as many as twenty-five thousand people to the town, easily accessible via the train. The area that Crystal Peak Park (Trail 4) now sits on memorializes that past.

Now, Verdi is a quiet getaway from the bursting metropolis of Reno, a great place to search for wildflowers among the Great Basin sagebrush and pines or to appreciate the golden beauty of fall cottonwoods. Although only two trails are listed in this section, they are very worthy of being included.

4 Crystal Peak Park Interpretive Trail

DISTANCE: 0.5-mile loop
ELEVATION GAIN: 50 feet
HIGH POINT: 4880 feet
DIFFICULTY: Easy
FITNESS: Walkers
FAMILY-FRIENDLY: Yes
DOG-FRIENDLY: Yes, leashed
AMENITIES: Benches, restrooms, barbecue grills, interpretive signs, historical markers, horseshoe area, water fountain
CONTACT: Washoe County, download map from website
GPS: 39.5151756°, -119.9952041°

GETTING THERE

Driving: From I-80 west, take exit 3 for Verdi. Turn left on South Verdi Road, then continue for 0.2 mile as the road turns into Crystal Park Road. After 0.4 mile, make a sharp left onto a paved road (you will see a sign for the park at the start of this road) and park in the lot (the lower parking lot). Alternatively, continue on Crystal Park Road for another 500 feet and park in the lot to the left (the upper parking lot).

Note: In winter, the lower parking lot is not maintained; park at the upper lot along Crystal Park Road.

Though short, this trail's 0.5 mile holds more than its weight in history and beauty. The park and adjoining trails are gorgeously draped along the Truckee River, making it the favored location for various pursuits over the last 150 years. The area was once the lavash Verdi Glen Resort, which invited guests with its pool, nightclub, and restaurant. Before that, Verdi Lumber Company operated on the land, harvesting and processing lumber for nearby mining towns and the railroad.

The ruins of Verdi Glen Resort's outdoor fireplace

The park's namesake, Crystal Peak, towers above on the west side of the river. This mountain provided crystal quartz for radio sets used in World War II. Various interpretive signs along the trail describe the ruins in detail. With all there is to see and enjoy, this short jaunt turns into a meaty daytime activity for people of any age.

GET MOVING

Access the dirt trail by walking north through the 3rd Street (or Business I-80) tunnel from the lower parking lot. Four trails fan out in a semicircle from west to east on the other side of the tunnel. Take the second from the left, which will begin the clockwise loop of the Crystal Peak Park Interpretive Trail.

Giant ponderosa pines—which have the same vanilla butterscotch scent as Jeffrey pines—welcome trail users and accompany them around the loop, along with incense cedar.

Looking west as the trail's loop nears its close

Their shade, mixed with the proximity of the river, make this a lovely trail even during summer. Slow down near one of the trees to see if you can get a whiff of that sweet smell.

The first historical marker lies at 0.1 mile and describes the ruins that come into view. Here are what remains of the Verdi Glen Resort's swimming pool and outdoor entertainment area, including the fountain, concrete foundation, and chimney. Continue a short way to find the first of two river access points. Be aware of the numerous social trails leading to the river and into the meadows. This area is sensitive and popular, and walking off the main trail can damage the environment.

The way now curves around and begins to head north. In about 0.1 mile, the next historical sign pops up, this time designating the Verdi Sawmill's mill pond. The trail heads through an area once used to store logs waiting to be processed. Now, only the calming sounds of the Truckee River and the deep green of the conifers adorn the trail.

In another 200 feet, arrive at the large cement foundation believed to be an abandoned addition to the Verdi Glen Resort.

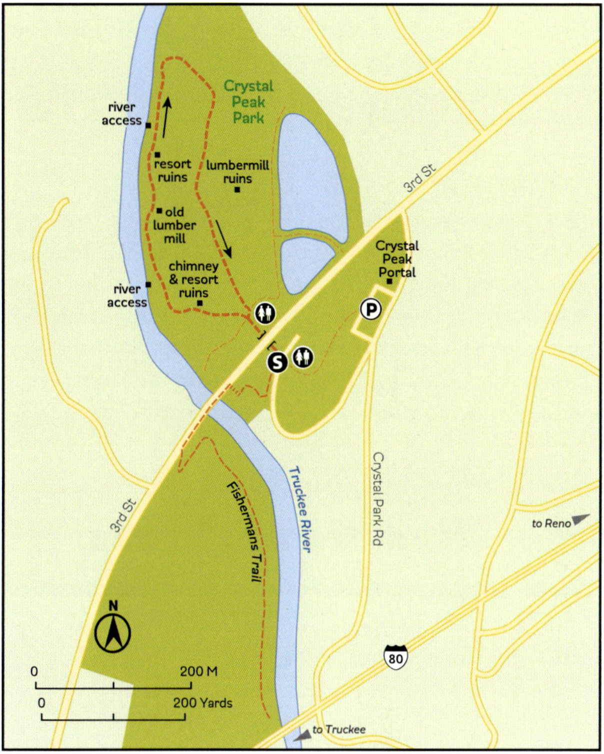

Continue through a small opening on the ruin's northeast wall. Here, at 0.3 mile, find the next river access point.

Continue straight (east) and enjoy the trickling of water as the Truckee makes its way toward Reno. The trail starts to loop back west, and views of Crystal Peak come into focus. Find the last historical marker at 0.4 mile, describing the ruins of the Verdi Lumber Company's dormitory, seen just off the trail. A final 0.1 mile completes the loop, ending at the tunnel.

Before you leave, make sure to visit the Crystal Peak Portal at the north end of the upper parking lot. Erected in 2019, this artwork is part of the Greater Washoe County ArTrail, which spans 200 miles from Verdi to Gerlach. The Crystal Peak Portal was created from native soil and rock and features the Washoe people's name for the area. Be sure to walk inside the structure to get a perfect view of Crystal Peak.

GO FARTHER

From Crystal Peak Park, the 0.8-mile Fisherman's Trail takes hikers west along the Truckee River. To access it, from the lower parking lot, take the stairs heading up to 3rd Street (Business I-80), where the road passes over the river, and find the protected walkway. Once on the other side of the river, continue about 100 feet to a small parking lot. From here, a well-designated trail winds down and along the river.

5 Verdi Nature Trails

DISTANCE:	0.5-mile loop
ELEVATION GAIN:	Minimal
HIGH POINT:	4900 feet
DIFFICULTY:	Easy
FITNESS:	Walkers
FAMILY-FRIENDLY:	Yes
DOG-FRIENDLY:	Yes, leashed
AMENITIES:	Pet waste stations, benches
CONTACT:	Nevada Department of Wildlife; maps available at on-site library
GPS:	39.521880°, -119.990727°
BEFORE YOU GO:	Area home to nesting wildlife; keep pets leashed at all times. Library open Tues. and Fri. 3–6 PM and Wed. 2:30–6 PM.

GETTING THERE

Driving: From I-80 west, take exit 3 for Verdi. Turn right off the freeway and follow Verdi Road for 0.4 mile. Turn left on Bridge Street. Continue for 0.3 mile, then turn right into the parking lot.

Enjoy the pines along the sandy path near the trailhead.

While this trail is easy, what it lacks in length, it makes up for in beauty and interest as it moves through shrub habitat to the edge of the pine forest. The trail is a unique collaboration between the Washoe County School District, Washoe County Library System, and Nevada Department of Wildlife to provide access to the outdoors, as well as a designated wildlife habitat study area.

Anytime of the year is nice for a walk along this trail, but be sure to visit in May and June to see wildflowers. The library does not need to be open for you to explore the trail, but it does offer free guides explaining the significance of the twenty-five trail markers. This guide transforms the walk into an educational exploration and a great way for children (and adults!) to learn more about their local environment.

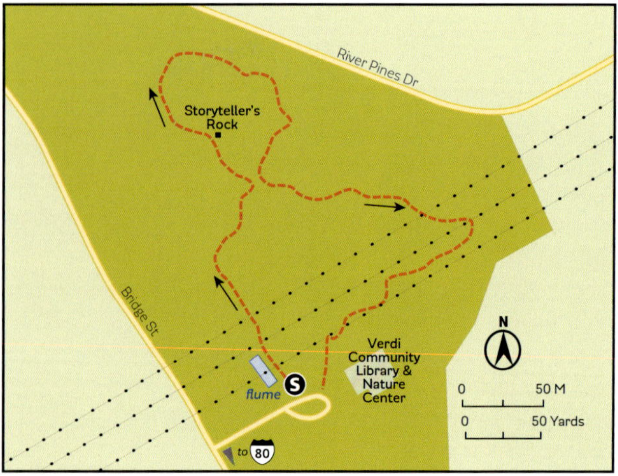

GET MOVING

On the north side of the parking lot, adjacent to the library, find the trail sign and pet waste station. It marks the beginning of the dirt trail, which starts in an upland shrub habitat spotted with antelope bitterbrush and Great Basin sagebrush, similar to other trails in the Reno/Sparks area.

Almost immediately, notice a wooden structure on the ground to the left (west). This is a flume used by the Verdi Volunteer Fire Station from 1920 to 1970. In about 300 feet, Jeffrey pine trees offer their signature vanilla-butterscotch scent and provide some shade in an otherwise exposed area. There is a tree close to the trail that you can sneak a whiff of. Put your nose close to the open fissures to see if you can pick up sweet notes!

At 0.1 mile, the two sides of the trail loop almost kiss, with both trails paralleling each other. Pay attention here, or you may end up on the southbound loop. Keep on the left (west) side of the bench and continue straight. In another 100 feet, the trail wraps around a giant granite boulder called Storyteller's Rock. With no other sizable rocks around to match, it makes the mind wonder . . . where did you come from? Likely, this rock traveled miles to this resting point, a slow tumble from seasonal snows and rains far above.

Ponder this over the next 100 feet as you continue north, before a beautiful open meadow opens up below and begs for attention. Rudimentary rock stairs lead down into this meadow, the lip of which (on the north side of River Pines Drive) seems to disappear into a little canyon before reappearing about 50 feet later. This valley houses the Truckee River. Be sure to take in the western edge of Peavine Mountain as the trail gently curves, before heading south through the meadow. You may notice a patch of mountainside that shines pink and orange from sedimentary rock, as substance that proves the area's marine past.

At 0.2 mile, notice some tall posts to help you navigate the trail. It can become overgrown here with grass during spring and early summer, though there should be evidence of previous footsteps trampling it down. After about 200 feet, the trail returns to the kissing spot, but this time, follow the southbound trail by keeping left (east). The next 0.2 mile wander out of the pine forest edge and back into the upland shrub habitat. During spring and early summer, California poppies grow here, adding a bright golden contrast to the rich greens and browns.

Although the trail brings you back near the starting point, it ends at a different spot in the parking lot than where it began—but it is only about 15 feet from your starting point.

GO FARTHER

If you've come all the way into Verdi from Reno, you might as well make your efforts worth it by tacking on an exploration of Crystal Peak Park (Trail 4) or the Verdi to Fleish Bridge (Trail 1).

Next page: *Peavine Mountain towers over North Valleys from the area's regional park (Trail 7).*

NORTH PEAVINE AND PAH RAH

North of Peavine and west of the great Pah Rah Range sits a smattering of communities, including Lemmon Valley, Panther Valley, Sun Valley, and Spanish Springs, as well as parts of Sparks. These communities lie outside of the Truckee Meadows, and peaks here shift and expand those glorious mountain views gifted to Reno. From here, the Basin and Range Province truly reveals itself, showing layered mountain ranges for as far as the eye can see. Read the "A State of Ranges" sidebar in Sugarloaf Peak Trail (Trail 11), for more details.

I admit, before researching this book, I wrote off this region as the growing pains of an exploding city and a drive that was way too far. That was a mistake. Hikes in this area are incredible ways to tap into nature, each providing experiences distinguished from one another. From the maze of trails and jaw-dropping views at Sun Valley to the birding haven at Swan Lake and the historic waltz of Wedekind Regional Park, there is something special waiting here. Development has climbed farther and farther north—even the trailhead of the northernmost trail in this book (Sugarloaf Peak, Trail 11) is accompanied by drywall and other signs of new buildings. Still, a sense of wildness accompanies the journey along these routes. Do yourself a favor: don't let Peavine block you from making the trek to explore.

6 Swan Lake Nature Study Area Trail

DISTANCE:	4.4 miles roundtrip
ELEVATION GAIN:	80 feet
HIGH POINT:	4950 feet
DIFFICULTY:	Easy
FITNESS:	Walkers
FAMILY-FRIENDLY:	Yes, boardwalk accessible for strollers
DOG-FRIENDLY:	No
AMENITIES:	Portable restroom, benches, picnic area
CONTACT:	Washoe County, download map from website
GPS:	39.650350°, -119.856724°
BEFORE YOU GO:	Open sunrise to sunset (hours posted at entry gate)

GETTING THERE

Public Transit: Take the RTC 7 to the Echo Avenue and Mount Charleston Street stop. Walk east on Echo Street for 0.4 mile, then turn left (north) onto Mount Limbo Street. Continue for 500 feet, where the trail opens up on the right.

Driving: From US Highway 395 north, take exit 74 toward Lemmon Drive. Keep right at the fork. Continue for 0.8 mile, then turn left onto Military Road. In 1.7 miles, turn right onto Lear Boulevard. Travel 0.4 mile, then turn left onto the Swan Lake Nature Study Area Driveway. Follow the road until it dead-ends in 0.2 mile at the parking area, sandwiched between industrial complexes.

Swan Lake is less like a trail and more like a slow adventure spotting wildlife. As a designated Important Bird Area, more than 150 bird species have been recorded in this area, including buffleheads, hawks, burrowing owls, and songbirds. The lake is best known for the migrating tundra swans from November to March.

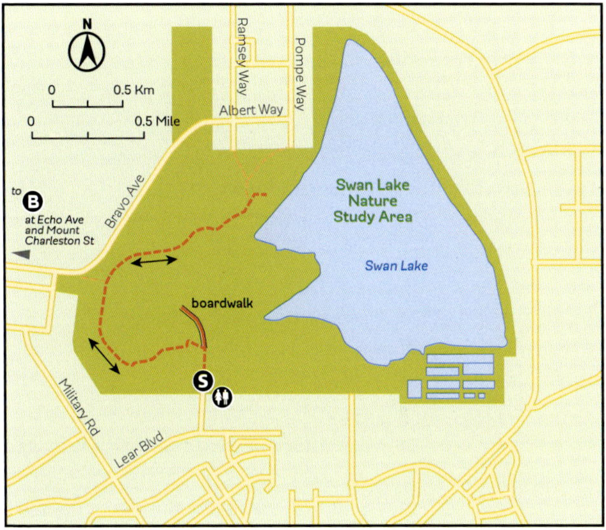

The wetland ranges from one hundred acres to one thousand, depending on seasonal precipitation. Trails are often submerged, and when not waterlogged, completely overgrown. But the main attraction isn't the shoreline, so don't be discouraged by reports of missing trails. The 600-foot-long boardwalk over the wetland is the jewel of the area, from willows and cottonwoods to forests of submerged cattails and burrs. The symphony of bird calls and their splashes of color in the lush growth take you into nature that feels so pure.

To get more out of your experience, join a Washoe County ranger-led event or a Lahontan Audubon Society event. Find more details on their websites.

GET MOVING

Although it might feel odd parking near industrial buildings, there is a large sign on the north side of the parking lot welcoming users to Swan Lake Nature Study Area.

Two trails split immediately from the trailhead. The right one takes users to the pavilion, visible just to the northeast. The left one heads north, toward a triangular information stand. Take this trail and make your way toward the sign.

The first 200 feet of this mixed-surface trail is exposed and travels through dry Great Basin sagebrush habitat. Occasionally, rabbits or reptiles cross the trail, and snake sightings have been reported. The walk transitions to denser riparian plants and trees the closer you come to the information stand, and the distraction of the human world begins to fade.

At 0.1 mile, arrive at a sign marking a major trail intersection. To the right (east) is a bridge and trail that leads to the pavilion and eventually the trailhead; to the left (west), the trail navigates the western shore of the lake. In front of you, in 300 feet, the pier begins, so continue straight. During the heat of summer, this 300-foot walk travels under overgrown willows that create a green tunnel nearly 8 feet tall. Take your time through here, as songbirds like the yellow-headed blackbird perch on plants, communicating without reserve. Here, you are insulated from the noises and sights of busy warehouses and roads nearby, allowing you to fully immerse yourself in the experience.

The pier zigzags out into the wetland for 0.2 mile. Interpretive signs provide information on the flora and fauna you might find here. In spots—during a wet year, especially—the pier rocks a little underfoot, but not so it seriously threatens your balance. In spring, make sure to look down to avoid stepping on goose droppings.

As you return to the intersection, make a right to head west. Here, a small metal fence opens to the side to allow entry. During wet years, you may walk as little as 400 feet before being stopped by water. If wet shoes don't bother you, continue, though you may have to navigate through dense overgrowth. The area can also be buggy.

Sunsets at Swan Lake are phenomenal, especially when summer flora decorates the landscape.

If passage is possible (and comfortable), continue westward for 0.6 mile. At 1 mile, a social trail shoots off to the north. Ignore it and stay on the same path for another 0.2 mile. Here the trail comes to a larger intersection. Take the northbound trail and continue along the wetland. Head straight for 0.2 mile, ignoring any small social trails.

At 1.4 miles, reach another junction. Here, four or five trails fan out. Take the second from the right to continue northeast. On this northern side of the park, people in off-road vehicles have created many interrupting trails. Continue northeast for 0.8 mile. A small vista trail veers off to the right, back toward the water. Take this short 200-foot extension to see more birds. When you're ready, retrace your steps back to the trailhead.

BIRD SCAVENGER HUNT

Test your bird knowledge with these eight seasonal visitors!

1. **Fall:** I kind of act like a duck, floating across the water, but my smaller, rounder body, black feathers, and white bill give me away as this patriotic bird.
2. **Fall:** Though my fallish colored neck gives me my name, the characteristic that best defines me is the spinning move I perform in the water—it helps me find food.
3. **Winter:** I hold my head up high as I glide across the water. You probably won't hear my "hoo-ho-hoo" call unless I am migrating, but my stark-white plumage and orange-spotted black beak should give me away.
4. **Winter:** Unlike my Canadian cousin, my feathers are usually white, though my coloration has morphed from completely gray to gray with a white face. Now, you will only see gray on my wingtips when I take flight.
5. **Spring:** I carry the name of a common bird, but boast a stunning coloration along my head and neck. You'll see me in the marshes and reeds but not on the water.
6. **Spring:** As I walk along the water, you will notice my long, thin legs and long, thin, slightly upturned beak. During breeding season, my grayish head and neck feathers turn a faint orange.
7. **Summer:** I have two bands of black feathers around my neck and tend to be vocal, singing a song that gives me my name.
8. **Summer:** I love walking at the lake's shore—you can tell by how my tail bobs and dances as I walk.

Answers: 1. American coot. 2. Red-necked phalarope. 3. Tundra swan. 4. Snow goose. 5. Yellow-headed blackbird. 6. American avocet. 7. Killdeer. 8. Spotted sandpiper.

(Photo of red-necked phalarope by Paul Horsley and Lauren Whitenack)

1

2

3

4

5

6

7

8

7 North Valleys Regional Park

DISTANCE: 2.4-mile loop
ELEVATION GAIN: 280 feet
HIGH POINT: 5250 feet
DIFFICULTY: Moderate
FITNESS: Walkers, hikers, runners, cyclists
FAMILY-FRIENDLY: Yes
DOG-FRIENDLY: Yes, leashed
AMENITIES: Pet waste stations, benches, restrooms, playground, soccer fields, skate park, barbecue area, picnic area, basketball and volleyball courts, horseshoe area, off-leash dog park, and hiking, biking, and equestrian trails
CONTACT: Washoe County, download map from website
GPS: 39.622168°, -119.864101°
BEFORE YOU GO: Open sunrise to sunset (hours posted at entry gate)

GETTING THERE

Public Transit: Take the RTC 7 to Sky Vista Parkway at North Valley Park stop. From here, you should see the parking lot with the trailhead.

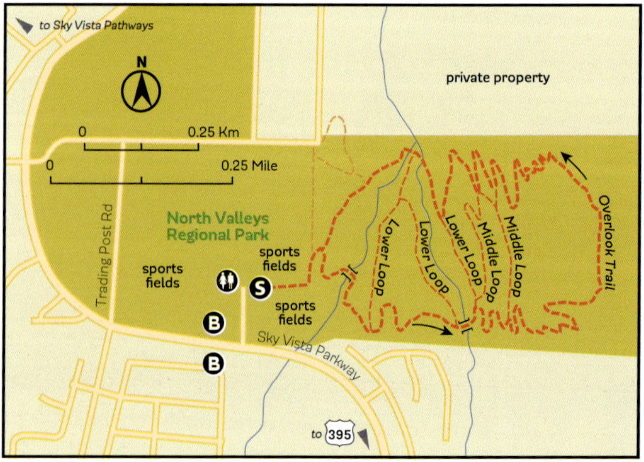

Driving: From US Highway 395 north, take exit 74 toward Lemmon Drive. Keep right at the fork. Continue for 0.2 mile, then turn left onto Sky Vista Parkway. Continue for 1.3 miles, then turn right into the parking lot.

Hikers new to North Valleys will notice the relentless series of switchbacks on this loop. While it does not disturb the experience, it can feel a bit silly. The trail design, however, serves an important function: this area was built to help mountain bikers progress their skills. The loop travels the perimeter of the three stacked levels of terrain that wind up the park's rocky hill. Easy trails line the base, intermediate in the middle, and challenging at the top. For hikers, this design makes little difference; the grade is gentle enough even toward the top.

Clearly, this area is popular with mountain bikers. Bicycle traffic should yield to pedestrians and be courteous to other trail users.

Connected to a regional park and a nearby neighborhood through a series of paved trails, this area is a stunning reminder that it should never be overlooked. The loop is great to hike year-round, though the yellow bitterbrush flowers make for quite the scene in spring.

GET MOVING

From the parking lot, locate the sidewalk that cuts between the baseball field on the north side of the lot and the soccer field directly east. The sidewalk turns into gravel before descending stairs to a wide gravel access road, leading north-south. Along this road are two trail signs and a bench. Walk to the farthest north sign to locate the start of the trail (which lines up near the midway point of the baseball field).

Almost immediately after joining the trail, another intersects it, running northeast and south. Make a right and double back south a little bit. The trail circumnavigates the park's three trails: the Lower Loop, Middle Loop, and Overlook Trail. They

Looking east while climbing the southern flank of the Overlook Trail

are rated as easy, intermediate, and hard, and each stay within their own elevation for mountain bikers, though these designations aren't so useful for hikers. This loop uses the outer rim of each to make a continuous journey.

Enjoy a soft dirt tread underfoot with very few loose rocks, an anomaly in Northern Nevada. Follow the trail about 0.1

mile to the first of two bridges. After crossing the bridge, the trail flirts with the park's boundary, and the adjoining neighborhood comes into view. The trail switches back a couple of times before meeting with another trail intersection at 0.3 mile. This north-south trail is one of the inner segments of the Lower Loop. Mark this, and other intersecting trails, in your mind for later—these make an excellent way to extend the route. For now, continue eastward.

At 0.5 mile, a north-south trail intersects, but continue straight. About 300 feet later, cross the second bridge. Take the northbound trail and follow it up the mountain for 200 feet. Here, make a right to switchback and head south, instead of taking the left side of the trail north. This is the start of the Middle Loop. The residential area fades from view, allowing you to focus on the amazing rock formations and antelope bitterbrush. At 0.7 mile, the rock formations are right along the trail. Right after the rocks, the trail switches back again (you'll hear that a lot on this trail) and then reaches the Overlook Trail. Over the next 0.6 mile, the trail gains about 200 feet of elevation.

This segment features beautiful views of the surrounding mountains, including Peavine to the southwest. During spring, find bright yellow flowering antelope bitterbrush all along the trail, especially pretty when framed by the rock formations.

At 1.1 miles, the trail reaches the ridge, where it gains another 50 feet in 0.2 mile—a welcome break from the uphill. The trail curves along the east side of the mountain, and new views unfurl eastward. Directly northeast of the trail is Swan Lake Nature Study Area (Trail 6). During spring and summer, notice the beautiful yellow flowers of the arrowleaf balsamroot, which barely shows itself on the west-facing slope. It looks very similar to the mule ear plant but is distinguished by its arrow-shaped leaves that aren't fuzzy like its cousin.

A bench at 1.3 miles marks the end of the elevation gain and the start of the downhill section as the trail wraps around to the west side of the mountain. Here, even more views—so far north and south!—pop out. Take a moment to sit, relax, and enjoy. Be warned of the descent: it is a dizzying journey through seventeen switchbacks that snap at each other rapid fire. By the end, you may swear off gradual slopes altogether.

After the trail makes its first turn from the summit bench, there will be ten switchbacks before it extends south and connects with the Middle Loop at 1.6 miles. Four switchbacks mark the meeting with the Lower Loop at 1.9 miles. At each of these junctions are trails extending straight south. Ignore these, follow through the switchback, and head north each time to continue this perimeter trail.

A small creek crossing (mostly dry during warmer months) interrupts the trail about 0.1 mile after connecting back to the Lower Loop. Another small crossing follows 140 feet later. This one might have some water in it, but it should be fairly low and easy to cross. After these two crossings, the trail rounds again and heads south. Here, you are finally done with the back-and-forth as the trailhead comes into sight. At 2.2 miles, a trail on the right leads to an alternative parking area. Ignore it and continue the last 400 feet, where you will exit the same way you came in.

GO FARTHER

While ascending or descending the Overlook Trail, explore the interior sections not covered in the loop trail above. Together, they will add nearly a mile to the journey, with about 100 feet more elevation gain.

Another option is the paved Sky Vista Pathways running through the adjacent neighborhood. Access them by walking west through the park and crossing Sky Vista Parkway where it meets the main entrance to the park. This trail network can add around 4 miles and under 100 feet of elevation gain to your experience.

8 Sun Valley Regional Park

DISTANCE:	2.1-mile loop
ELEVATION GAIN:	220 feet
HIGH POINT:	5170 feet
DIFFICULTY:	Moderate to challenging
FITNESS:	Walkers, hikers, runners, cyclists
FAMILY-FRIENDLY:	Yes
DOG-FRIENDLY:	Yes, leashed
AMENITIES:	Restrooms, picnic benches, disc golf course, pet waste stations
CONTACT:	Washoe County, download map from website
GPS:	39.611888°, -119.786638°
BEFORE YOU GO:	Navigation is tricky; bring a map. Northern and western park boundaries border BLM land; OHV users and target shooters recreate here. Open 8 AM to sunset (hours posted at entry gate).

GETTING THERE

Public Transit: Take the RTC 5 to the Sun Valley Boulevard and Middle Fork Drive stop. Walk southeast on Sun Valley Boulevard for 140 feet to Middle Fork Drive. Turn right and continue 240 feet on Middle Fork Drive, then turn left onto Amargosa Drive until it dead-ends at the park, about 0.1 mile.

Driving: From US Highway 395 north, take exit 70B for Clear Acre Lane toward Sun Valley. In 0.4 mile, merge onto NV 443. Continue for 3 miles, then turn left on West 7th Avenue and make first right onto Sidehill Drive. Continue for 0.5 mile, then turn left where the road dead-ends. Continue for 0.4 mile to the parking lot; continue past an overflow lot and then park at the end of the road.

One of the prettiest in the region, Sun Valley Regional Park is not your typical park. Instead of grassy fields and playgrounds, it features open space, many trails for hikers and cyclists, and a disc golf course. Hikers here can get jaw-dropping views of layered mountains framed with rabbitbrush, Utah juniper, and ancient granite boulder outcrops—without having to climb steep terrain. The area can be difficult to navigate, as trails weave and overlap, but don't let that deter you. Come with snacks, plenty of water, a sense of adventure . . . and patience. Hiking here can be great for the whole family, but maybe get your bearings before introducing the kids.

The loop described here runs through the center of the 343-acre park. Use this as a rough guide to inspire further exploration. Locate landmarks to help you navigate, and take the trails that speak to you.

GET MOVING

This loop starts on the gorgeous Sun Rock Trail. It is the only well-marked trail and the easiest to follow in the park, a great introduction to the area's beauty. From the parking lot, locate the dirt trail to the left of the restroom. Head northeast for 0.1 mile, where a sign points left (northwest) for the Sun Rock Trail. Continue about 150 feet, then make another left, heading southwest for 0.2 mile. Ignore any trails heading directly north-south. As you walk, look for information signs and benches along this segment.

From here, random outcrops of rock decorate the trail. These granodiorite formations are a stunning reminder of the area's impressive geologic history. Here, magma cooled under the earth's surface, forming quartz crystals. Granodiorite, very simply, is differentiated from granite by the amount of quartz present (granodiorite contains less). One of the informational signs notes that these are 40-million-year-old rocks, but local geologists date them to the Cretaceous period, forming about 90 to 100 million years ago.

At 0.3 mile, the trail turns south to a more open area. It winds a few times, finally straightening out at 0.4 mile to a wide-open trail. After 0.5 mile, reach a gravel lot. Walk north

Enjoying mountain vistas to the east among rubber rabbitbrush and Utah junipers

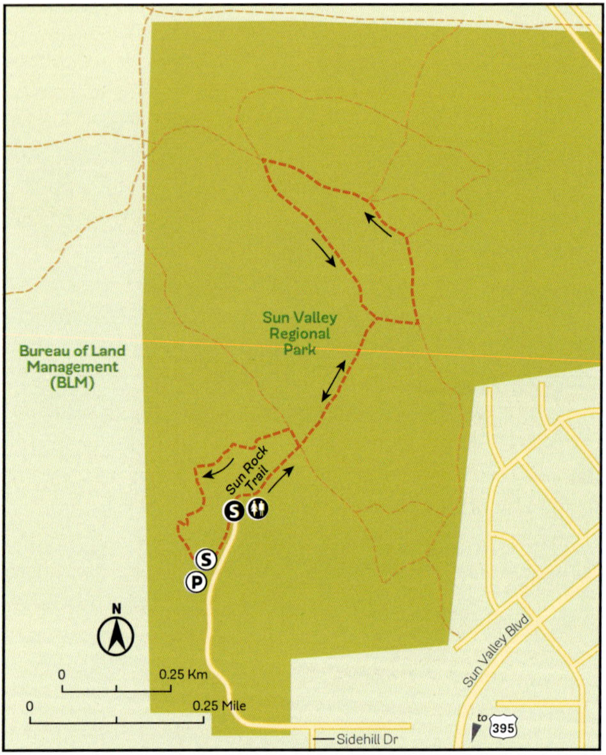

along the road for about 0.1 mile, returning to the paved parking lot. While a bit redundant, start at the same trailhead again, and walk the same path 0.1 mile to the Sun Rock Trail sign. This time, continue straight. After 100 feet, the trail meets the bike park trail junction. Ignore it and continue straight.

Along this stretch, Utah junipers line the trail, their branches full of the characteristic bright blue berries. In early spring, bright pink desert peach, phlox, and paintbrush speckle this truly stunning landscape, made only better by the views that begin to show themselves to the east. At 0.9 mile, dip into and out of a dry yet very rutted gully. From this point, the trail changes from wide and easy to one with loose rock; watch your footing as well as your direction. There is also a change of environment. A maze of trails and dry washes takes over, each easily confused for this route. Stay patient, have your map handy, and open your mind to a beautiful adventure.

About 0.1 mile down the trail from this gully, notice a wooden fence—there are several of these that help mark the trail. Soon, reach a large intersection with a major east-west trail. Make a right to head east toward the fence (about 300 feet), then turn left to head north. This straight-away reaches another fence in 650 feet. Turn left, where you'll find a wide-open area with signs of bike use. It can be hard to distinguish what trail to follow here, so do your best to continue on a northwest trail. Others might look convincing, but the correct one should not make any sharp turns north or south.

After 0.2 mile, come to another complex intersection. Three trails lead northwest, and one switches back southeast. Take the southeast one. If you come to a fence, you missed the switchback and have gone too far west. Round the switch-back, then head straight southeast along the path. In about 0.2 mile, the trail crosses a dry wash, where it looks like there is a trail that continues straight. Instead, make a slight right and take the trail that heads south. Follow it for about 120 feet, then turn right, heading east to return to the base of the loop in 170 feet. This should bring you back to the straight-away trail that connects the Sun Rock Loop to this upper loop. Head south back to the trailhead. You've made it!

GO FARTHER

There is a whole network of trails here, though they aren't necessarily easy to follow, and some force hikers under the fence separating the nonmotorized park and the mixed-use Bureau of Land Management land. For a full map of trails, visit the Washoe County website.

9 Wedekind Regional Park

DISTANCE: 3.3-mile loop
ELEVATION GAIN: 380 feet
HIGH POINT: 4740 feet
DIFFICULTY: Moderate
FITNESS: Walking, hiking, running, cycling
FAMILY-FRIENDLY: Yes
DOG-FRIENDLY: Yes, dogs may be off leash but under control.
AMENITIES: Portable restroom, pet waste station
CONTACT: City of Sparks Parks and Recreation, download map from website
GPS: 39.57469°, -119.74362°
BEFORE YOU GO: Open sunrise to sunset (hours posted at entry gate)

GETTING THERE

Driving: From I-80 east, take exit 18 to merge onto NV 445 north (Pyramid Way). Turn left off the freeway to stay on Pyramid Way. Continue for 3 miles. Turn right onto Disc Drive, then make your first right into the trailhead parking lot.

Though a major freeway runs beneath it and a shopping complex crowns its north end, the buzzing world fades from the lookout at Wedekind. Visit during sunrise or sunset to see the sunlight wash a spectacular gold over the horizon and a soft pink on the mountains. One of the only open spaces within the city of Sparks, Wedekind offers multiple lookout points and an open range for off-leash dogs to hike with their owners.

It is also a site along the Washoe County ArTrail, a link of cultural, historical, and artistic landmarks from Verdi to Gerlach. Wedekind was chosen because of its history with mining. From the lookout point adjacent to the 4th Street trailhead, you can see the site of the former mine across Pyramid Highway. See the Go Farther section to learn more.

The origin of the piles of rock that sporadically decorate the trails at Wedekind Park is a mystery to local park and trail officials.

GET MOVING

Locate the trailhead at the south end of the parking lot, where three trails spur off. Take the one immediately to the right (west). The middle trail will also deposit you in the same spot, so if you take it by mistake, you will be all right.

After about 200 feet, the trail dead-ends at an old paved road. Turn left to head south here. This "trail" is actually what is left of old Nevada State Route 33, which connected Pyramid Lake to Interstate 80. It has since been replaced with Pyramid Highway (Nevada State Route 445). At 0.3 mile, the trail curves around to the west and the pavement fades into dirt. Continue west for about 150 feet, past a small, fenced utility area. The trail forks here; stay right to take the northern prong and continue west for 0.1 mile, keeping the lookout peak to your right.

When a fence running parallel to Pyramid Highway comes into view, look north along the flank of the mountain to find a skinny northbound trail. It can be hard to see during spring growth, but that season brings with it tall grass riffling in the wind, causing the mountainside to come alive. About 640 feet after joining this trail, it switches back briefly south before curving around the hillside and summiting the mountain.

Though Pyramid Highway sits below, a stunning view overwhelms the rush of traffic. Beyond the immediate rust-red rock and soft grasses, the Truckee Meadows take shape. To the east, make out the dip of the Truckee River that defines the southern boundary of the Pah Rah Range and the northern boundary of the Virginia Range. Straight ahead, Huffaker Hills block the grid of neighborhoods, with Mount Rose standing above it all. Enjoy the view and solace.

Take the same route in reverse back down to where the dirt and pavement meet. About 300 feet east of this point, notice trail signs that distinguish trails by color, correlated with the trail's difficulty. A sign points to a green trail heading east and a blue trail heading south. Follow the blue trail. This section continues the brilliance of the peak, providing views south through the Truckee Meadows, even as far as the Jobs Peaks that tower over Eagle Valley. At 1.3 miles, ignore the trail spurring southwest and continue south for another 100 feet. Here, three trails fan out. Take the rightmost (southwestern-bound) trail. The way becomes rocky here, so mind your step.

At 1.6 miles, the trail turns east before resuming a familiar southbound direction after 170 feet; do not take the trails that continue east here. About 230 feet later, the trail makes an abrupt turn east and begins going around the mountainside. At 2 miles, find a sign for the red or blue trail. Choose the red, or easternmost, one, which only gains about another 30 feet of elevation. Continue for 0.25 mile, then follow the trail west toward the power plant.

Walk another 0.1 mile before coming face-to-face with the structure and a major junction. Take the trail on the right (eastern) side of the power plant; it should be straight across from where the red trail ended. Though it disrupts the serenity of nature, the time spent walking around this structure is short-lived. Keep your focus on the creek bed that borders the trail on the right. Here, the bright green, fluttering leaves of the cottonwoods make it feel like a completely different trail than the red rock one leading to the peak.

At 2.5 miles, follow the trail that goes right, around the eastern perimeter of the hill, keeping the creek bed on your right. A small pasture appears beyond the creek, and the

Traversing the grassy slopes of Wedekind Park

gentle mooing of cows accompanies the walk. The last and final junction is easy to miss. At 2.7 miles, look closely for a trail heading left (west). If you miss it, you will end up on a trail with a rock wall, leading to the shopping center. Continue straight for the last 0.5 mile, arriving back to the parking lot.

GO FARTHER

Wedekind Park has more than 4.5 miles of trails. To get a look at the Wedekind mine, climb to the lookout point via a 0.3-mile loop. From the 4th Street parking lot, walk east along the trail, crossing Orr Ditch and landing at the picnic pavilion. Walk south along the eastern side of the hill. A small trail diverts west from here, leading to the top. From the peak, look across Pyramid Highway to the light-colored hilltops. This was the location of the mine.

10 Sparks Regional Trail System

DISTANCE:	4.2 miles roundtrip
ELEVATION GAIN:	50 feet
HIGH POINT:	4520 feet
DIFFICULTY:	Easy
FITNESS:	Walkers, runners, cyclists
FAMILY-FRIENDLY:	Yes, ADA and stroller accessible
DOG-FRIENDLY:	Yes, leashed
AMENITIES:	Pet waste stations, benches; restrooms at Golden Eagle Regional Park; picnic area at Bitterbrush Park
CONTACT:	Wingfield Springs HOA (no official map)
GPS:	39.595831°, -119.668224°
BEFORE YOU GO:	There is an open shooting range south of the Pah Rah Interpretive Trail into Spanish Springs Canyon.

GETTING THERE

Driving: From I-80 east, take exit 21 for Greg Street toward Vista Boulevard, and turn left from the exit. Continue for 8 miles. Turn right on Homerun Drive, then immediately go left on Touchdown Drive. Make the third left into the youth baseball field's parking lot.

This lollipop-style roundtrip trail is a combination of the Golden Eagle Regional Park trails, Sparks Regional Trail System, and old golf course trails. Cyclists should be mindful of pedestrians on these narrow, paved trails. When heading south, the route looks directly into the beautiful Spanish Springs Canyon of the Pah Rah Range, lining the eastern and southern edges of this area. Its name is a Paiute term, translated into Lake Mountain, referring to Pyramid Lake. Though the Pah Rahs do extend to Pyramid Lake, early surveyors confused them with the range along the lake's western shore, now called the Virginia Mountains. This is poor naming all around,

The ponds along this section of Sparks Regional Trail System are an urban oasis for birds.

as the Pah Rah Range is bordered to the north by the Virginia Mountains and to the south by the Virginia Range.

This path introduces you to the Sparks Regional Trail System, which meanders through neighborhoods and connects to parks and natural features. Learn more in Go Farther below.

GET MOVING

From the parking lot, the northernmost in the park, walk 0.3 mile to Vista Boulevard by accessing the sidewalk on the south side of the parking lot. Cross Vista Boulevard north, and then cross again to the west.

This might seem unusual because the route approaches a neighborhood. However, after walking 0.2 mile west on Vista Boulevard, a path appears on the right. As you continue, the mountains to the north and west begin to reveal themselves along with the beautifully manicured landscaping. Trees on the path provide shade when they fill out in spring. At 0.9 mile, a trail opens up to the right (east) just as the main trail begins to curve east as well. Turn right here, and after 150

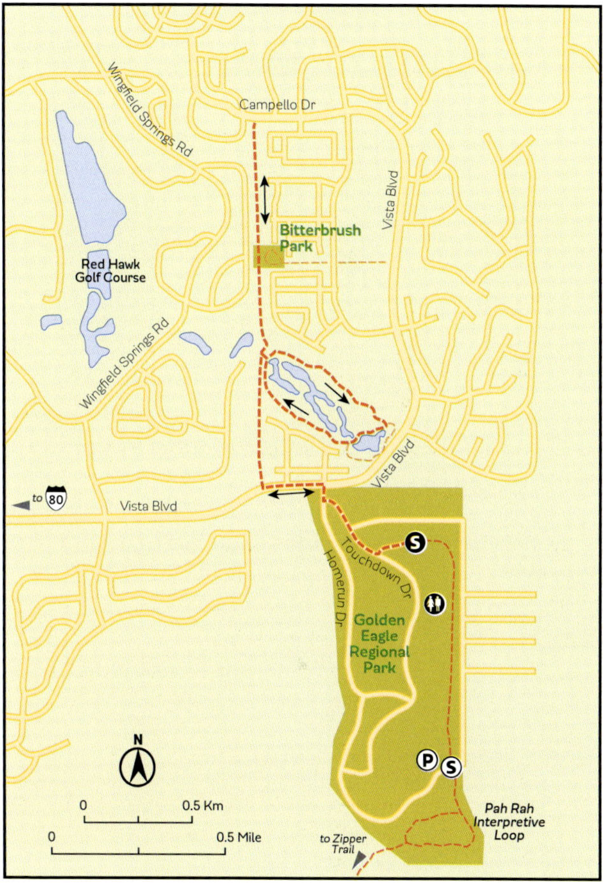

feet, reach a pond. Head clockwise around the ponds, which creates a 1-mile loop. Here, find giant stalks of cattails, tall grasses, and healthy Great Basin sagebrush where birds flit around. Many make their homes here, such as red-winged blackbirds, coots, and belted kingfishers. A symphony of songs fills the air, almost hiding that this trail is bordered by a neighborhood and a golf course.

A STATE OF RANGES

The view from Sugarloaf Peak shows why Nevada is so unique. It has more mountain ranges than any other state in the country—314 named ranges and some unnamed ones. They are formed by the opposing motions of the Pacific Plate (moving northwest) and North American Plate (moving southwest) that create the Basin and Range Province. Look at a topographic map from Lake Tahoe to Utah's Wasatch Range; you'll see parallel ranges generally 10 miles wide and 80 miles long, spaced between valleys.

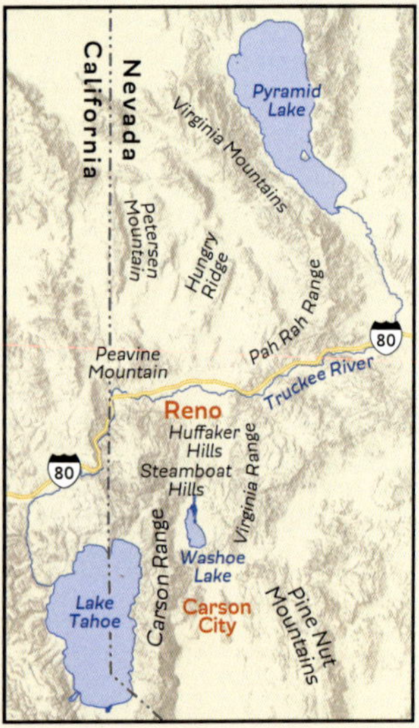

The ranges and major mountains surrounding Reno, Sparks, and Spanish Springs

To visualize this, local geologist Rachel Micander said to stretch out a piece of dried playdough and notice the fractures that occur as you pull. "Along those fractures," she says, "the land [or basins] drops down relative to the ranges." It is hard to conceptualize the mountains and land beneath us changing. But through plate movement and seismic activity (Nevada is the third most seismically active state), it moves every day, extending about the size of a basketball court every year. In fact, the ranges around us—Carson, Peavine, Virginia, and Pah Rah—weren't formed until about three million years ago.

From Sugarloaf Peak, how many ranges and peaks can you count?

At 1.3 miles, the loop reaches its southeastern point and turns to head west. Take a right here. (Another paved path continues straight and makes its way around the last pond, but it doesn't fully connect on the pond's other side.) Along this 0.1 mile stretch of the loop, the trail goes between two

A slice of tranquility between Sparks's neighborhoods

ponds, allowing you to get pretty close to each. At the end of this stretch, make another right to continue clockwise. Again, ignore the paved path that turns left (south) from here and makes a false loop around the last pond.

Complete the loop trail at 1.8 miles and meet back with the main trail. Turn right (east) and continue here. The trail curves around briefly before straightening back out north. At 2.1 miles, there is access to Bitterbrush Park—with a good grassy spot, playground, and picnic area—on the eastern side of the trail. There are no restrooms here, but it makes for a great place to stop and take a minute to rest.The trail meets with Campello Drive at 2.6 miles. Here, choose to retrace your steps back to Golden Eagle Regional Park, or extend your time by continuing on one of the other neighborhood paths.

GO FARTHER

There are many ways to extend this jaunt. Walk south through Golden Eagle Regional Park to the 0.5-mile Pah Rah Interpretive Loop, where tumbleweeds tangle with Great Basin sagebrush and gunshots echo from adjacent Bureau of Land Management (BLM) land. For more, connect to Zipper Trail into Spanish Springs Canyon, which ascends nearly 1000 feet in 3.2 miles. This does go through a designated open shooting range, and some trail reviews note disrespectful shooters.

Or travel a less jarring journey through more of the Sparks Regional Trail System, which boasts more than 20 miles of trails (and growing!). A nice route goes from Red Hawk Golf Course to the Kiley Wetlands. Note: pedestrians must stay off golf course cart paths when golf is in play.

11 Sugarloaf Peak

DISTANCE:	5.5 miles roundtrip
ELEVATION GAIN:	810 feet
HIGH POINT:	5290 feet
DIFFICULTY:	Moderate
FITNESS:	Walkers, hikers, runners
FAMILY-FRIENDLY:	Yes, but some steep sections with loose rock
DOG-FRIENDLY:	Yes, leashed
AMENITIES:	Pet waste stations
CONTACT:	Washoe County, download map from website
GPS:	39.67538°, -119.69826°
BEFORE YOU GO:	Exposed trail; watch for rattlesnakes

GETTING THERE

Driving: From I-80 east, take exit 18 for NV 445 north (Pyramid Way). Turn left from the exit and continue on Pyramid Way for 10.4 miles. Turn right on Horizon View Avenue and continue for 0.1 mile, then make the first right onto Paradise View Drive. Trailhead parking is at the end of the road in a cul-de-sac, in about 0.1 mile.

Sugarloaf inspires the heads-down, push-to-the-top hiking that may make you question trekking it at all. When the trail really starts to climb, it zigzags more than 500 feet up, stumbling over rocks and stealing lung capacity. Up until the final

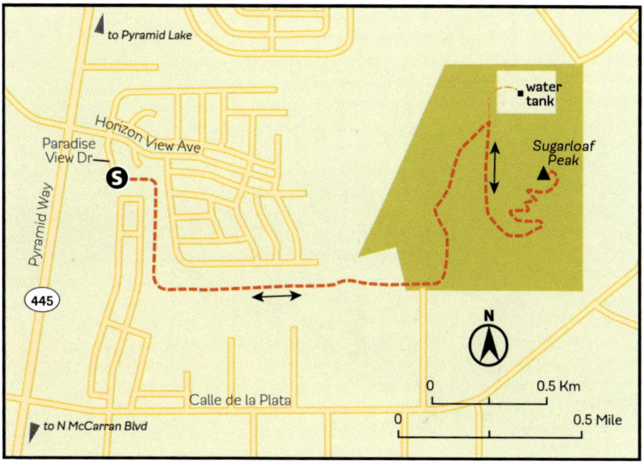

switchback, the desire to get to the top comes from the pure stubbornness not to quit after getting *this far*.

But as that final switchback rounds the peak of Sugarloaf, you realize that this spot, dotted with paintbrush and flowering hopsage, boasts views of the dozen or so mountain ranges that grace this pocket of Northern Nevada, which Renoites rarely get to see—from the snow-covered distant peaks of Freel, Jobs, and Jobs Sister standing above Eagle Valley, to the northern reaches of the Pah Rah Range. Visit in winter through late spring to see the mountains in their glory, but fall can be nice too.

GET MOVING

To find the trail, look to the south, behind the wood fence lining the cul-de-sac, and locate a trail sign pointing east. Walk 300 feet, then cross a gravel access road and resume on a sandy path behind another wooden fence.

The first 1.2 miles travel between neighborhoods and along private property. Throughout this section, numerous neighborhood access trails join with this one. The trail is well marked and easy to differentiate from these spurs, but if

A thunderstorm moves toward Sugarloaf Peak from the north. Always check the forecast before you begin an adventure!

you do make a wrong turn, you won't walk far before hitting asphalt and realizing your mistake. The first of these neighborhood trails connects at 0.1 mile, where your path makes a sharp right to the south. The second and third come at 0.4 mile. Here, the featured trail turns sharply left to the east. The fourth enters at 0.7 mile, and the fifth and final at 0.9 mile.

At 1.2 miles, the trail dead-ends at a red fence. Carefully zigzag through the gate here, and notice another trail sign pointing users to the left. This sign is premature, noting how the trail eventually moves in about 300 feet. Go straight until then, where the trail naturally turns left (north). There shouldn't be any other trail or road here to sway your directional decision.

After you make this turn, the trail is very easy to follow. It gains noticeable elevation—about 130 feet in the next 0.5 mile. Don't be too discouraged by the towering Sugarloaf Peak standing to the right of the trail. As you make this brief climb, the mountains to the west and north begin to reveal themselves. Sagebrush is interrupted here and there with sunflowers, Utah junipers, and the tiny white flowers strung along flatcrown buckwheat during May. At 1.8 miles, take a sharp right onto a much smaller trail at a marked intersection.

Here is where the fun begins. Get ready for a 480-foot ascent in just under a mile. If a breeze is in the air, be prepared for it to multiply to a roaring wind as you sway up the mountainside to the peak. Don't let this dissuade you; there is an amazing view waiting at the top. On this winding 0.9-mile uphill section, be sure to mind your feet. Sharp basalt and loose rock litter the trail. This rock can make it difficult for pets, so you may consider protecting your dog's paws with booties for this stretch.

At 2.1 miles, this southbound section curves around to the east and switches back six times before landing at the peak. Each whiplash switchback gains just under 70 feet. Pace yourself here, and if you begin to feel hopeless, direct your gaze to the beautiful views of the Sierra and Virginia Ranges to the south, instead of up at the remaining ascent.

Finally, at 2.7 miles, you've reached the summit of Sugarloaf Peak! Take your time (after you catch your breath) to enjoy the sweeping panorama. Here, outside the bowl of Reno, the views are much more expansive. From the mountains towering over Eagle Valley to the northern reaches of the Sierra and Pah Rah Ranges, it's a fairy-tale patchwork of peaks. In spring, take time to search the Great Basin sagebrush for paintbrush, more sunflowers, and flowering hopsage, and keep an eye out for the occasional hawk or desert horned lizard.

Once you've enjoyed the splendors of the peak, head back the same way to the trailhead.

Next page: *The famous N, representing the University of Nevada, Reno, is a prominent feature along Trails 15 and 16.*

NORTHWEST RENO

Peavine Mountain, standing at 8269 feet, sets the stage for many of the northwest Reno trails. Thanks to dedicated volunteer organizations like Biggest Little Trail Stewardship, there is no shortage of nonmotorized trails on the mountain itself. A smattering of motorized roads intersects and parallels the trails, connecting users to the northern and western sides of the mountain.

Sitting on the southeastern side of the mountain is Washoe County's largest regional park: Rancho San Rafael. Containing an arboretum, dog park, and extensive trail system (with an access tunnel under McCarran Boulevard), it makes a great jumping-off point for ready explorers or those who require paved paths and want to enjoy the splendor of Peavine.

Because this side of town was built more recently—around the 1980s and '90s—neighborhood pathways were part of the planning and include miles of paved paths connecting homes with public space. Rainbow Ridge to Las Brisas (Trail 13) is one part of this system. Because this nook of town sits at a higher elevation than downtown Reno, exceptional views can be found even from level hikes like Sierra Vista Park (Trail 12).

Between the vast network at Peavine Mountain, the enormity of Rancho San Rafael, and the neighborhood pathways, there is a little something for everyone in this section.

12 Sierra Vista Park

DISTANCE: 1.8-mile loop
ELEVATION GAIN: 220 feet
HIGH POINT: 5310 feet
DIFFICULTY: Easy to moderate
FITNESS: Walkers, hikers, runners, cyclists
FAMILY-FRIENDLY: Yes, trails are open to bikes, so be aware.
DOG-FRIENDLY: Yes, leashed
AMENITIES: Interpretive signs, porta potties, pet waste station, bench (at trailhead only), bike repair station
CONTACT: City of Reno, download map from Biggest Little Trail Stewardship
GPS: 39.533531°, -119.902414°
BEFORE YOU GO: Open sunrise to sunset (hours posted at entry gate). Trail borders private property, so be aware and respectful and keep children and pets close.

GETTING THERE

Driving: From I-80 west, take exit 9 for Robb Drive. Make the first left onto Sharlands Avenue and continue for 0.6 mile. Turn right onto Avenida de Landa, and continue for 0.8 mile. Turn left on Beaumont Parkway and continue for 0.4 mile, before making the final left into the park via Clubhouse Drive.

Stunning 200-acre Sierra Vista Park is one of Reno's newest, opening in 2019 and transforming the former Northgate Golf Course into a haven of trails for hikers and cyclists. This isn't a typical park, but rather an open plateau of hiking trails, mountain bike trails, and pump tracks. Possibly the best feature is the incredible view. From here, trail users can see south across the river basin to the mountains above Hunter Creek Falls, west to Crystal Peak, and north to Peavine Mountain.

Interpretive signs explain the natural environment, helping users appreciate the vegetation, including antelope bitterbrush,

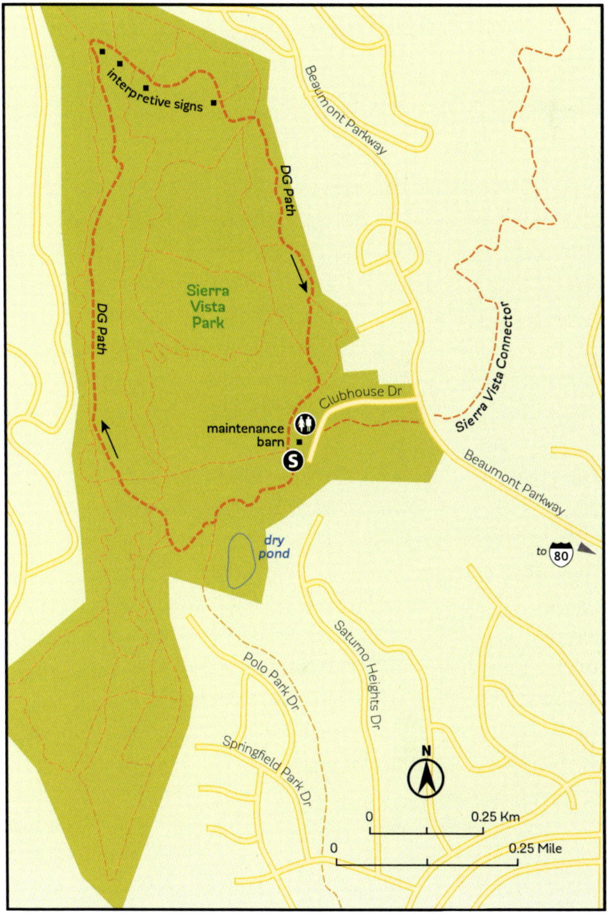

Fremont cottonwood, Great Basin sagebrush, and rubber rabbitbrush. Early morning hikers may even catch sight of a cottontail rabbit or two. This park is lovely to visit any time, but nights and weekends can get pretty busy. The trail is exposed to both sun and wind; be mindful of the weather before attempting to hike.

This trail's difficulty is listed as moderate for the potentially tricky navigation, as there are many intercepting routes within the park.

GET MOVING

Locate the large maintenance barn on the west side of the parking lot, and walk south along the eastern side of the barn until you reach a sandy trail and a wooden fence. Technically, the trail runs along the barn's west side, but the jumble of other trails back there makes it a confusing starting point. Of the many trails in this park, the DG Path is the only one that maintains its width and sandy consistency—a contrast to the strip-thin bike paths that intercept here and there.

From this entry point, walk south about 50 feet until the trail turns westward into the vast landscape of the park and toward gorgeous views of Verdi. Likely, a few cyclists can be seen racing around the park's inner tracks—fun entertainment while enjoying this nature-filled hike.

At 0.1 mile, the trail forks. Keep left. In another 50 feet, an intersection connects the DG Path to the Sierra Vista Rock Art Trail heading south (see Go Farther), a cart path heading directly west, and several mountain biking trails heading north. Again, the DG Path will be distinct in both the consistency and color of trail (light sand) and width. Continue straight (southwest).

The pine-tufted hills of Peavine extend to the north of the trail, and walking along this path looks as if the hillside runs right into the speckled evergreen mountainside. At 0.6 mile, as the trail turns to the north, encounter another tricky intersection. Here, three paths appear to fork off the main trail, remaining parallel to the DG Path. Stick to the one in the middle and continue.

As you head north, dark green bitterbrush stands out in the mix of dusty sage and tall grasses. In May, the desert peach glows pink here, and in fall, rabbitbrush speckles the

Peavine Mountain turns gold under dramatic lighting on a stormy day.

land with gold. This is one of the great benefits of visiting a trail throughout the year—the environment is constantly changing.

At 0.8 mile, find the first interpretive sign. There are four total, each covering a unique feature of the park. This first one explains transforming the area from golf course to park. In another 0.2 mile is the second interpretive sign, this one noting the vegetation of the area.

At 1.1 miles, the trail intersects the Old Asphalt Golf Cart Path, which continues north and runs along the property line of nearby homes. To stay on the DG Path, head to the right (east). There are three trails connecting the Old Asphalt Golf

Looking west over wintering rubber rabbitbrush with Crystal Peak towering in the background

Cart Path and DG Path along the next 0.2 mile, which will run into the DG Path perpendicularly at 1.1 miles, 1.2 miles, and 1.3 miles. Again, these trails are easily distinguished from the DG Path because they are much thinner and rockier.

Look for the last two interpretive signs, depicting wildlife and wildfire, near 1.2 and 1.3 miles. At 1.4 miles, make a sharp right to stay on the DG Path. From here, a simple 0.4-mile walk south will bring you back to the trailhead. When you are 0.1 mile from the trailhead, another wayward cart path might tempt you toward the left, but stay straight and finish the trail at the parking lot.

GO FARTHER

A nice way to extend this hike is by taking the Sierra Vista Connector. This trail is included in Rainbow Ridge to Las Brisas (Trail 13), as it connects to many of the other neighborhood paths in the area. From the park, it is a 1.9-mile journey with little elevation gain to Las Brisas Boulevard, which can then connect to the endless adventure of Peavine nonmotorized trails (like Trails 14 and 15).

13 Rainbow Ridge to Las Brisas

DISTANCE: 4.3-miles roundtrip
ELEVATION GAIN: 375 feet
HIGH POINT: 5220 feet
DIFFICULTY: Easy
FITNESS: Walkers, runners, cyclists
FAMILY-FRIENDLY: Yes, ADA and stroller accessible
DOG-FRIENDLY: Yes, leashed
AMENITIES: Pet waste stations, trash cans, benches, interpretive signs, seasonal restrooms, basketball courts, playground equipment
CONTACT: City of Reno (no official map)
GPS: 39.526405°, -119.874167°
BEFORE YOU GO: Frequent snake sightings; keep young children and pets close

GETTING THERE

Public Transit: The RTC 4 services the Northwest neighborhoods. The closest stop is Robb Drive at Canyon Creek Park. From here, head north 0.1 mile, then turn right (east) onto Simons Drive. Continue for 0.4 mile until you reach Rainbow Ridge Park.

Driving: From I-80 west, use the second from right lane to take exit 10 for North McCarran Boulevard West and turn right onto McCarran. In about 0.2 mile, make the first left onto Sierra Highlands Drive, then take the first left onto Simons Drive and continue for 0.6 mile. Turn left on Rainbow Ridge Road and park alongside the park on the street.

The Northwest Neighborhood Network links hundreds of homes in northwest Reno to parks (Rainbow Ridge, Sierra Vista, Canyon Creek Park, Terrace Sports Complex, and Valley Wood) and Peavine Mountain. While not all sections of the neighborhood network connect without briefly hopping on a sidewalk, these trails are amazing ways to get moving.

The section from Rainbow Ridge Park to the La Brisas trailhead is described below. It frequently crosses roads that may or may not have crosswalks, and it backs up to private property at some points; please be respectful. The delightful 4.3-mile trail traverses Robb Canyon and links neighborhoods to the Northwest Public Library and Peavine Mountain Trail network. It ascends 375 feet, reaching its highest point at 5220 feet. In spring, search Rainbow Ridge for Palmer's penstemon, a tall plant with delicate pink flowers.

GET MOVING

From Rainbow Ridge Road, locate the paved trail on the west side of the grassy slope. Continue south about 620 feet to the trail intersection. The path on the left leads to a playground, basketball courts, picnic tables, and seasonal restrooms and water. Continue straight.

After a pleasant 165-foot walk past Russian olive trees on the left and ornamental trees on the right, the trail switches back to the north, making an M of switchbacks down to and over a creek. Soon after, the trail makes another switchback. Native plants—Great Basin sagebrush, rabbitbrush, and antelope bitterbrush—replace grass here as the path enters the Robb Drive Drain, which houses Chalk Creek. The remaining 2 miles of the journey out follow this creek. At the end of this switchback, Chalk Creek trickles under the trail, adding to the tranquility of this verdant area.

Continue for 100 feet and turn right at the dirt trail, the final turn of the M-shaped trail. The pale, chalk-like sandstone slope to the left characterizes this section; its diatomaceous rock, featuring the silica shells of microscopic plankton, is evidence of an ancient lake or slow-moving river. Here, Chalk Creek comes into clear view, along with a greater variety of steppe plants and flowers. Watch for early morning bunnies, scampering quail, and the occasional snake crossing the trail.

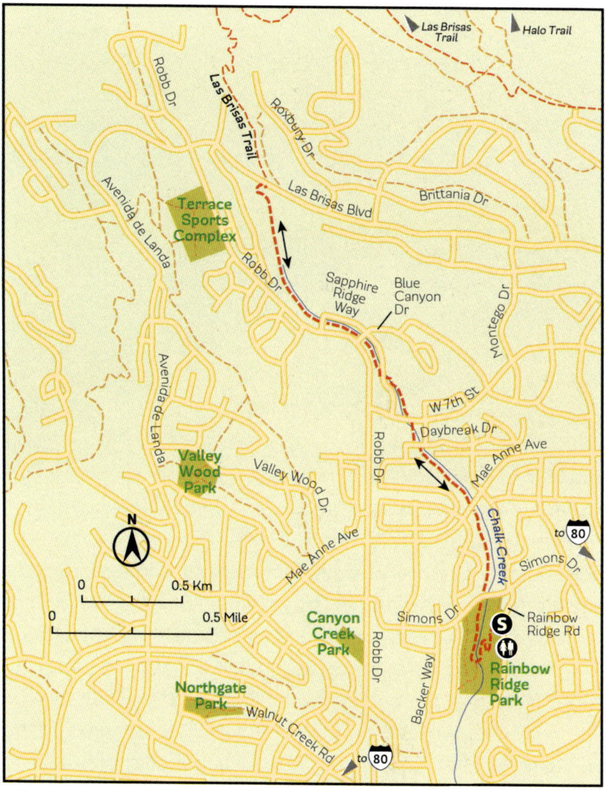

The dirt path undulates as it makes its way to Simons Drive, gaining about 50 feet overall.

Cross Simons Drive with caution; morning and afternoon traffic can be hectic. The trail traverses six more roads, some major crossings and some quiet neighborhood ones. The number of roads, and the rapid succession of reading about them, may feel more arduous in this trail description than it will in person. Stick with me here and continue on the paved path for 0.3 mile, until Mae Anne Avenue intersects the trail.

Looking toward the Carson Range, a spur of the greater Sierra Nevada

Though there is a crosswalk with a pedestrian light, traffic moves fast along this road. Cross with caution.

Continue straight on this paved path for 0.2 mile. Cross Daybreak Drive at 1.1 miles and follow it west for about 30 feet until the trail begins again. Continue on this path for 350 feet, then cross West 7th Street. The trail continues for 800 feet before crossing Sapphire Ridge Way. Head north on Sapphire Ridge about 20 feet before meeting with the paved trail again (on the left). Follow it for 650 feet, then cross Blue Canyon Drive. Continue 600 feet and cross Sapphire Ridge Way again at 1.6 miles for your final (woohoo!) road crossing.

At this point, the trail deviates from houses and opens up to an unbothered stream basin of sagebrush. As the trail ascends 150 feet on its final 0.6-mile journey, the wilderness of Peavine Mountain takes over your vision. This trail, in fact, ends at the Las Brisas trailhead, an entryway to the network of nonmotorized Peavine trails. Enjoy the views as the trail approaches La Brisas Boulevard, where it ends. Contemplate extending your hike, or follow the same steps in reverse to return to Rainbow Ridge Park.

GO FARTHER

The Las Brisas Trail is a great way to add extra miles to the Rainbow Ridge walk. This 6-mile roundtrip trail makes a total ascent of 290 feet, climbing into the Peavine foothills and connecting to many other trails. Though you may not spot other hikers, this area is very popular with mountain bikers. Be courteous and step off trail to let them pass.

14 East Keystone Canyon Loop

DISTANCE: 4.4-mile loop
ELEVATION GAIN: 600 feet
HIGH POINT: 5500 feet
DIFFICULTY: Moderate to challenging
FITNESS: Walkers, hikers, runners, cyclists
FAMILY-FRIENDLY: Yes
DOG-FRIENDLY: Yes, leashed
AMENITIES: Pet waste stations, benches, portable restroom
CONTACT: Washoe County, download map from Biggest Little Trail Stewardship
GPS: 39.551221°, -119.848964°
BEFORE YOU GO: Watch for snakes; area is very popular with mountain bikers and adjacent trails are popular with motorized users; let bikers pass; be mindful of trail crossings.

GETTING THERE

Public Transit: The closest option is RTC 7 for the North Virginia Street and North McCarran Boulevard stop. To access the trail from there, walk to McCarran and make a right to follow it west for 1.1 miles. Turn right on Leadership Parkway and follow it for 0.3 mile, where a sign for the East Keystone

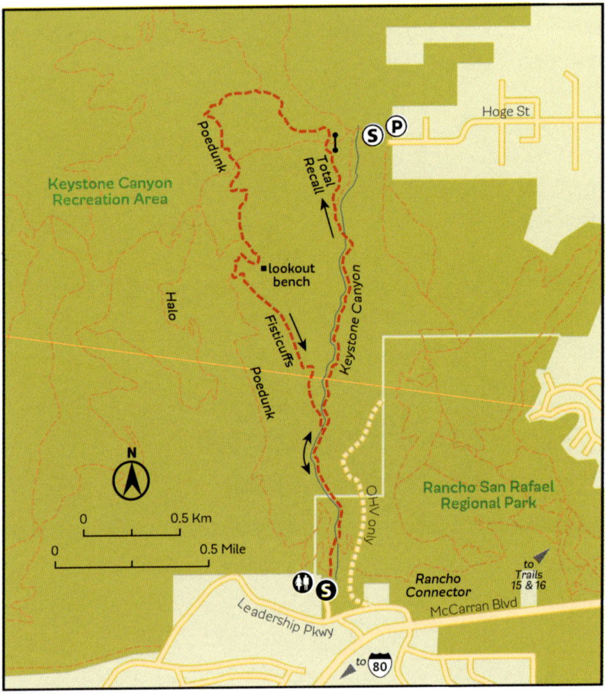

Canyon trailhead parking lot appears on the right. Follow the sign and turn into the parking lot to access the trail. Another option is to use the 1-mile Rancho Connector trail, which can be accessed through the Evans Canyon trailhead.

Driving: From North McCarran Boulevard, turn north onto Leadership Parkway. Continue for 0.3 mile, then make a left at the stop sign. Take the first right in 420 feet (this is easy to miss) at the sign for East Keystone Canyon trailhead to enter the parking lot.

Keystone Canyon is a popular jumping-off point to explore the southern side of Peavine Mountain, where there are 50 miles of nonmotorized trails and even more motorized ones splintering off throughout the hillside. From far away, Peavine looks like a monotonous hillside, but there are canyons, pockets of wildflowers, groves of pine, and seasonal creeks. Each trail reveals new sights.

This trail is popular with trail runners and mountain bikers. Mornings seem to attract less bike traffic, but be aware of your surroundings. Late April through early June is the best time to find wildflowers here. While most of Peavine is exposed (morning and evening hiking is best), Keystone Canyon enjoys cover from sun about two hours before sunset, offering a way to get outside even during summer.

Major intersections of this trail system are well-marked. This loop follows the Keystone Canyon, Total Recall, Poedunk, and Fisticuffs Trails. Note that snakes have been sighted in this area and OHV trails intersect nonmotorized trails in some areas.

GET MOVING

Locate the trail on the north side of the parking lot, just beyond the portable restroom. Initially, the trail is flanked by an apartment complex to the west and a creek bed to the east. Though water does flow here, it is seasonal and mostly dry by June. As you reach the northern boundary of the apartment complex (about 260 feet from the trailhead), another trail extends northwest up the hillside; ignore it, as well as a similar intersection that occurs at 0.1 mile. When in doubt, remember that the Keystone Trail is wide and maintains a steady pace along the creek bed.

Each step farther along the trail reveals a greater variety of foliage. During May, pink hopsage, desert peach, three-petaled mariposa lily, and purple Dorr's sage decorate Keystone Canyon, with the occasional pop of paintbrush and sunflower. Aspens shimmer in the summer breeze, and bright yellow sweetclover and rubber rabbitbrush extend the canyon's color through fall. The rest of the year, this environment is defined by dry grasses, Russian olive, and Great Basin sagebrush.

At 0.6 mile, the trail meets the Fisticuffs Trail, which will complete the lollipop loop—but for now, stick to Keystone Canyon.

After this junction, the Keystone Canyon Trail gets closer to the creek. Here, the trail is very thin in some spots, with a steep slope extending to the creek. Watch your footing, especially as the trail becomes rougher with buried rock. The closer you are to the creek, the greater you immerse yourself in the stunning foliage. In this environment, how many different flowers, shrubs, and trees can you count? Reference the Guide to Common Native Flora in the beginning of the book to help you.

In 1.3 miles, reach the end of the trail's first 250-foot elevation gain and the junction with the Total Recall Trail. Here, turn left to join Total Recall. After 0.4 mile, a fence cuts through the landscape, but there is an obvious gap for hikers to continue through. After crossing this line, the trail enters a wide, open area. Continue straight about 200 feet, then turn left (west) at a trail sign to continue on Total Recall.

Leaving the creek canyon reveals a different vision of Peavine, with layers of hills, some topped with small groves of pine trees. Notice the many trails (some sanctioned for motorized use) that cross this area and feel the thrill of future adventures brewing. The Hoge Street trailhead can be seen from here too, marked by a small utility building to the east.

At 2 miles, reach a road and follow it for about 130 feet until you come to the next one. These roads are open to motorized use; be aware of fast-moving vehicles. Cross this second road and look for the trail sign marking where the Total Recall Trail picks back up. In 260 feet, the trail splits. Here, make a slight left to join the Poedunk Trail as it extends west. After 0.3 mile, the trail curves around and begins to head south. The elevation gain here is more noticeable than the gradual gain throughout the canyon.

WILDFLOWER CHECKLIST

Nevada's state flower is Great Basin sagebrush (also called big sagebrush), but many more blooms can be found in the Truckee Meadows. From April to July, how many of the following flowers can you find along Evans Creek? Each month gives way to new blooms, creating a different backdrop each time. Find pictures of these either on iNaturalist or in the Guide to Common Native Flora in the beginning of the book.

- ☐ Antelope bitterbrush
- ☐ Arrowleaf balsamroot
- ☐ Desert peach
- ☐ Dorr's sage
- ☐ Great Basin muilla
- ☐ Hopsage
- ☐ Lupine
- ☐ Mariposa lily
- ☐ Narrowleaf milkweed
- ☐ Paintbrush
- ☐ Palmer's penstemon
- ☐ Rough eyelashweed
- ☐ Shaggy milkvetch
- ☐ Thistle
- ☐ Twinleaf onion
- ☐ Waxy checkerbloom
- ☐ Whitedaisy tidytips
- ☐ Woods' rose

When you've gone 2.5 miles total, pause the uphill struggle and capture a great view of downtown Reno to the southeast. From here, you can see the Pah Rah Range, Virginia Range, and the peaks of Mount Rose above the Peavine foothills. At 2.6 miles, the trail splits. Continue on the Poedunk Trail. From here, a bench should come into view. Walk about 300 feet from the last junction to reach it. Sit for a while, enjoy the view, and appreciate the conclusion of the climb.

When you're ready to get moving again, continue on the Poedunk Trail. At 3.1 miles, keep left at the trail junction to join the Fisticuffs Trail, which has a steep descent with some loose rocks. Watch your step and take your time along this 0.7-mile stretch. The trail passes around a cool rock formation at 3.7 miles. On the other side of this, Keystone Canyon comes back into view. Join the Keystone Canyon Trail at 3.8 miles and follow it back to the trailhead.

Looking northeast during a spectacular sunset

GO FARTHER

The chance for discovery is endless here! An easy extension is to continue along Total Recall instead of joining Poedunk at the 2-mile mark. Follow this for 0.6 mile, then join the Halo Trail, which winds west of Poedunk through the hills. It meets back with the lollipop loop 300 feet north of the overlook bench (connecting Halo to Snow Terrace at 3.1 miles), adding a total of 3.7 miles and 640 feet of elevation gain.

15 Evans and Vista Loop

DISTANCE: 4.1-mile loop
ELEVATION GAIN: 1020 feet
HIGH POINT: 5290 feet
DIFFICULTY: Moderate to challenging
FITNESS: Walkers, hikers, runners, cyclists (prohibited on Nature Trail)
FAMILY-FRIENDLY: Yes, some steep sections with loose rock
DOG-FRIENDLY: Yes, leashed
AMENITIES: Portable restrooms, benches, pet waste station, trash cans
CONTACT: Peavine Mountain Trail Network, download map from Biggest Little Trail Stewardship
GPS: 39.553917°, -119.829556°

GETTING THERE

Public Transit: Take the RTC 7 to North Virginia Street at the Reno Sports Complex. From here, turn right into the sports complex parking lot and continue to the far northwest corner to access the trailhead.

Driving: From I-80 east, take exit 13 for Virginia Street and make the first left on Sierra Street. Drive for 1.1 miles north, then turn left onto Virginia. Continue north for 0.4 mile, then turn left after McCarran Boulevard into the Reno Sports Complex parking lot.

Keystone and Evans Canyons are part of the greater Peavine Mountain Trail Network, which dominates northern Reno. It is jointly managed by the City of Reno, Washoe County, and the US Forest Service. The N that shines from this part of the trail stands for University of Nevada (Reno), a beacon seen from around town. This section is also notable for the Basque Monument, which commemorates sheepherders from Northern Spain who immigrated to the area in the late 1800s and left a lasting impact on Northern Nevada culture.

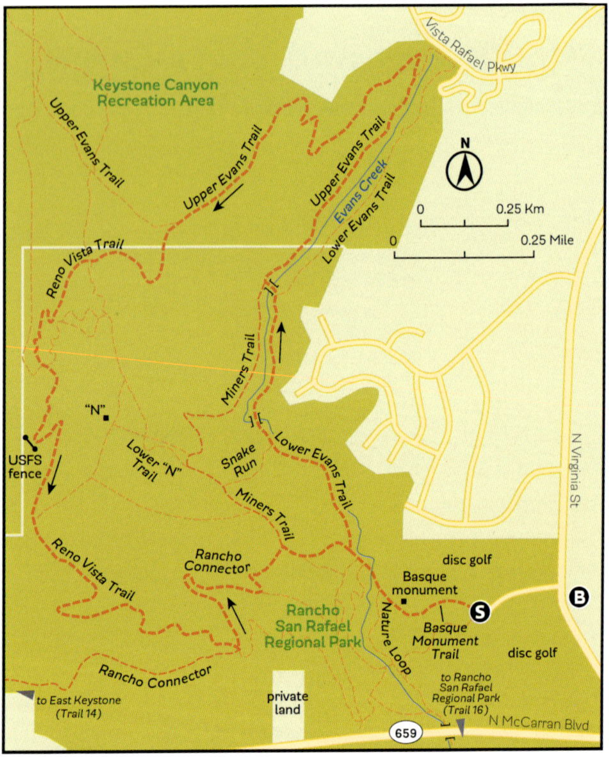

The area is popular with cyclists. Though bicycle traffic should yield to pedestrians, watch for them and be cautious and courteous to all trail users. Keep dogs and young children close. Note that cycling is prohibited on the Nature Trail; cyclists should use the Keystone East trailhead and approach the trail via the Rancho Connector. The trail is exposed to both sun and wind; be mindful of the weather before you go.

GET MOVING

To access the trailhead, locate the signs at the northwest side of the Reno Sports Complex parking lot. Several disc golf trails

Though civilization is close, this trail feels quiet.

splinter to the left and right. Take the wide, west-facing trail in the center of this commotion. In 450 feet, the distinctive turquoise Basque Monument comes into view. If you would like to get a closer look, it is an easy off-trail addition. Otherwise, go about 100 feet, cross a small footbridge, and keep right at the next trail intersection.

Soon, cross Evans Creek. The depth depends on the time of year and the intensity of winter. Continue straight (north) from here for another 200 feet, where the trail opens up and reveals another maze of routes. Locate Evans Canyon Trail, the farthest trail on the left (east) and the only one that follows the creek, and take it.

At 0.6 mile, continue straight at the trail junction with the Snake Run trail. Then turn left (north) at 0.9 mile on a roughly 20-foot-long trail that crosses the creek and connects to the Miners Trail, at an intersection marked with a trail sign. Once across the creek, make a right to head northeast. Continue for another 0.5 mile where the trail splits. Keep left. Continue straight for another 370 feet. It will look like you are heading toward the Vista Rafael Parkway road, but the trail switches back southwest and begins to climb the hill. From this point (1.4 miles) to the end of the three switchbacks (2.2 miles), the route climbs 360 feet.

As you make this ascent, red rock formations come into view. This is an example of quartz-rich volcanic rock that was altered by geothermal waters millions of years ago. The reddish-brown color comes from iron-oxide minerals within the rock. Similar rock can be found along the Hunter Creek Falls Trail (Trail 20). A local geologist notes that small cavities within the rocks show small quartz crystals.

About 50 feet from where the trail meets the top of the climb (2.2 miles), the trail splits at a trail marker. Take the left trail for the Reno Vista Trail. In another 0.2 mile, the trail comes to a prominent intersection. The other trails (UNR DH and UNR DH Alt) run north/south. Continue straight (west) to stay on the Reno Vista Trail. In the next 0.3 mile, the trail switchbacks six times as it makes its final climb of about 100 feet of elevation gain. After the final switchback, the trail reaches another intersection at 2.8 miles—this time with the Upper N Trail. Continue straight (south) as you look out to the downtown Reno skyline.

Loose rocks litter the trail as it begins to descend next. Be mindful of your steps. At 3.2 miles, continue straight (south) at a marked trail intersection. In about 140 feet, a fence appears on the right (west) of the trail, as do two other trails heading south. Stay on the trail in the middle—not the one hugging the fence or the one leading southeast.

The trail loses 370 feet over the next 0.8 mile. The Reno Vista Trail snakes in loose switchbacks down this slope. Count eight, then turn left at 3.7 miles to join the Rancho Connector Trail. Continue for 0.3 mile around the switchbacks, then make the first available left turn at 4.1 miles. Make the first right after 650 feet to join the Miner's Trail. In another 600 feet, the trail merges with the Basque Monument Trail, which brings you back to the trailhead.

NO TOMATOES UNTIL PEAVINE SAYS GO

Peavine Mountain stands at the northwest end of Reno, separating it from Sun Valley, North Valleys, and Cold Springs. Topped with radio towers, it is distinguishable from nearly every pocket of town. However, its reputation does not rest solely on its grandeur. Instead, the crowning peak draws our eyes to help us predict the weather.

There is an old saying still whispered around town today that the 8269-foot peak determines the perfect time to plant tomatoes and other garden goods. The theory is that if there are temperatures cold enough to keep snow on Peavine, it is a certainty that frost will ruin your delicate tomato plants.

This lore might get a chuckle out of longtime Renoites, who have most likely heard this tale for decades. These are the same people who have seen snow fall on the Fourth of July and raging winters keep their snowy grip on the peak well into summer. Springtime here usually brings a hopeful warm front, followed by a late freeze and cold spurt, so if you are planting tomatoes this spring, maybe start them inside and wait for consistent temperatures.

Mighty Peavine Mountain under the pink hues of sunset

Nearing the summit on Upper Evans Trail

GO FARTHER

This area is home to many trails. Not only does this trailhead connect to Rancho San Rafael Regional Park (see Trail 16), but it also connects to Keystone Canyon and greater Peavine Mountain trails (see Trail 14) to the west. Access the Keystone Canyon Trail via the Rancho Connector Trail. If starting from the southern end of the Reno Vista Trail, travel for 0.8 mile before turning right onto the Keystone Canyon Trail. Hike 0.8 mile and ascend 300 feet to the top.

If you want to make this journey around Evans Creek shorter, a great option is to cross over to the Miners Trail at 0.8 mile, then loop back to the Evans Canyon Trail via Snake Run. This is a 2.3-mile loop with 230 feet of elevation gain and a favorite from late April through June for incredible wildflowers.

16 Rancho San Rafael Regional Park

DISTANCE:	3.2-mile loop
ELEVATION GAIN:	260 feet
HIGH POINT:	4730 feet
DIFFICULTY:	Easy
FITNESS:	Walkers, hikers, runners, cyclists (prohibited on Arboretum Loop and Nature Trail)
FAMILY-FRIENDLY:	Yes
DOG-FRIENDLY:	Prohibited on Arboretum Loop; leashed dogs allowed on other park trails
AMENITIES:	Restroom, playground, off-leash dog park, volleyball court, horseshoe area, exercise area, picnic area, barbecues, tables and benches
CONTACT:	Washoe County, download map from website
GPS:	39.545958°, -119.825193°
BEFORE YOU GO:	Open sunrise to sunset (hours posted at entrance); gates locked when closed

GETTING THERE

Public Transit: Take the RTC 17 to the North Virginia Street and North McCarran Boulevard stop. From here, cross McCarran and continue for 440 feet. Make a slight right toward Sierra Street and continue walking south for 0.3 mile. Turn right on Putnam Drive and walk 470 feet. Here, keep right as Putnam becomes San Rafael Drive. Continue for 0.2 mile, then turn right into the trailhead parking lot.

Driving: From the intersection of Virginia (US Business 395) and North McCarran Boulevard, head south on Virginia and keep right to fork onto Sierra Street. After 0.4 mile, turn right onto Putnam Drive and continue for about 500 feet before turning right into the trailhead parking lot.

Rancho San Rafael Regional Park is the county's largest at 580 acres. It includes a lovely park with a playground, grassy spots, and picnic areas, and it extends north across McCarran to include the Evans and Vista Loop (Trail 15). This loop combines the Arboretum Loop, Evans Creek Trail, Nature Trail, Pasture Loop, and South Park Loop, offering a great baseline to understand the primary park trails and be inspired to explore further.

While in the park, be sure to stop at Herman's Pond to view birds and walk through the Nevada Farm & Families Area, where farm equipment, turkeys and chickens, and a pollinator and community garden are located—perfect for families to explore! Also at the trailhead, find the Wilbur D. May Museum, which houses artifacts, special exhibits, and events. Check the Washoe County website for current exhibits.

GET MOVING

This mixed-surface trail starts with the Arboretum Loop. Locate the west entrance at the northeast side of the parking lot, marked with a large wrought iron gate and sign, to the left of the Wilbur D. May Museum. If the pup is joining you, skip this loop and instead start along the Pasture Loop. (To get there, walk toward the Arboretum trailhead, but instead of turning right to enter the arboretum, continue straight for 0.2 mile to the northern end of Herman's Pond. Here, turn right to head east for 200 feet. The Arboretum Loop joins at the next junction. Turn left to head north here, then follow the directions below.)

For the Arboretum Loop (see detail map on page 128), enter at the gate and travel through the Davids Grove Conifer Collection. At the first junction, choose which side of the loop you'd rather see: Take a left and enjoy the Native, Rock, and Shade Gardens and Maple Grove along the north side. Or go right and enjoy the Rose Garden and Dixie's Plaza Garden along the south side.

This first loop ends at the Xeriscape and Songbird Garden (at 490 feet southbound or 540 feet northbound). Follow the trail south to the Kleiner Oak Grove and meander as the

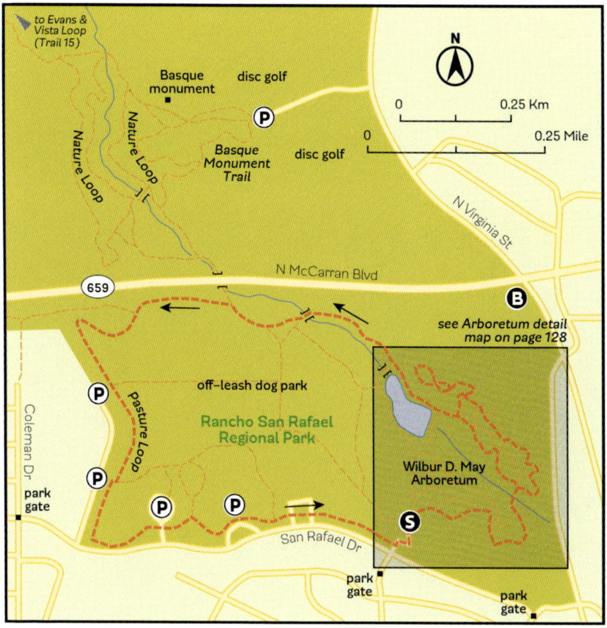

trail loops toward the east and then back north. At 0.2 mile, at the Blakely Conifer Garden, continue to the right toward Evans Creek and May Grove. Cross Evans Creek on a lovely boardwalk. Here, nearly sixty bird species can be seen in a single season. Enjoy delightful shade and the relaxing sound of the burbling creek on one of several benches under a pergola near the bridge.

About 75 feet along the trail, it splits into the upper loop. Go right toward Potter Grove, where the trail splits again about 300 feet later. Within the next 500 feet, the trail splits three more times; keep right at each to stay on the main loop. In this section, the trail passes through Potter Grove and Fannie's Garden, then around Bree Megan's Grove and Dwight Grove to the beautiful Irwin Overlook at 0.7 mile. This is the highest point on the trail and rewards visitors with a beautiful

A lovely spot in Wilbur D. May Arboretum's Rose Garden to stop and take in the beauty

vista. Look out across Herman's Pond, Evans Creek, and the pasture west, toward the towering Sierra Nevada.

Continue for about 740 feet, where the trail splits. Take the trail to the right, leading to Herman's Pond and the Pasture Loop on a wide, sandy path (see main trail map). Along the pond, look for waterfowl and other birds. At 1 mile, at the northern end of the pond, continue straight. Dog walkers: here's where you join again.

At 1.2 miles, cross a wetland on a sturdy boardwalk, listening for a cacophony of birds, including the red-winged blackbird. Continue another 0.1 mile along the northernmost trail. Here, notice a tunnel decorated with murals traveling under North McCarran Boulevard. Turn right and walk through the tunnel, which leads to the Nature Loop on the north side of the park. You can also access the Evans and Vista Loop (Trail 15).

Out of the tunnel, notice a well-defined trail heading straight (northwest), a smaller trail to the left, and a social trail on the right. Continue straight. At 1.4 miles, reach another junction and continue straight (north) onto the Nature Loop. Here the trail is domed by cottonwoods and willows. Overgrown plants like nightshade and Russian olive mix with sage, desert peach, and rubber rabbitbrush. It is a sanctuary (if you ignore the bugs) that feels miles away from the busy four-lane road. At 1.7 miles, the trail loops back around and begins its journey south. Continue 0.3 mile in this wetland paradise. At 2 miles, head left (east) to connect back to the trail leading to the tunnel, walking another 0.3 mile through it and rejoining the Pasture Loop.

Here, turn right to head west on the Pasture Loop Trail, gaining about 60 feet over the next 0.1 mile around the off-leash dog park. A fence separates it from the trail. At 2.3 miles, a trail heads right, connecting to a dirt parking lot. Continue straight (south), keeping the dog park on your left. The entrance to the dog park is at 2.5 miles, and the fence is open here. While dogs should be leashed from the park to the parking lot, they may not be.

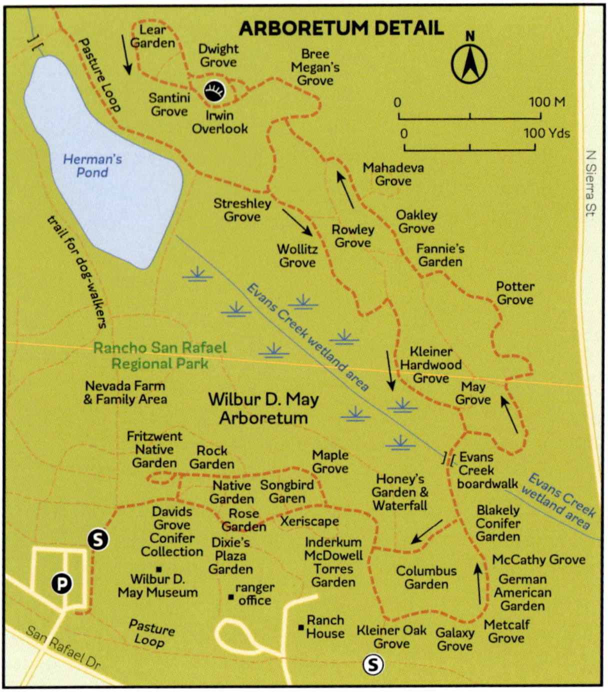

Continue south past the dog park entrance. At 2.7 miles, you pass a trail leading east that bisects the park and is a lovely option, but for now, continue straight for another 400 feet before heading east. This side of the trail parallels San Rafael Drive, returning to the parking lot in 0.5 mile. Though near the road and with the potential to be accosted by geese, this leg of the trail is nice because it walks under beautiful trees and over miniature creeks.

GO FARTHER

Extend this loop by connecting the Evans and Vista Loop (Trail 15) to the Nature Loop on the north side of North McCarran Boulevard. From the northern tip of the Nature Loop, continue

View west toward Mount Rose with the greater expanse of Rancho San Rafael Regional Park in the foreground

north across the creek, keeping to the easternmost side of the large open area just beyond.

If you want to add on a smaller trek, explore the areas of the Arboretum that were overlooked in the trail description above. One could easily spend hours wandering and appreciating more than four thousand plant species across nearly 23 acres.

Next page: *Beautiful fall colors along the Truckee River at Oxbow Nature Study Area (Trail 17)*

SOUTHWEST RENO

Southwest Reno is defined by the breathtaking Carson Range, which includes the highest mountain in Truckee Meadows (Mount Rose at 10,785 feet) and the highest mountain in the Tahoe basin (Freel Peak, 10,886 feet). The Carson Range is technically a spur of the Sierra Nevada Mountain range, separated by small faults. Within the northern reaches of the range is the Mount Rose Wilderness, a 30,000-acre area containing its namesake mountain. This wilderness runs along Southwest Reno and is broken into two sections, bisected by Hunter Lake Road (see Cold Canyon Loop, Trail 21). The northern section can be experienced along Hunter Creek Falls (Trail 20).

The area is also defined by the Truckee River and the ditches cut from it, such as Steamboat Ditch (Trail 22). Westward expansion and gold discoveries changed the local climate. Farmers began growing alfalfa to support ranchers, and soon, ditches like the Last Chance Ditch and Lake Ditch crossing Bartley Ranch (Trail 24) diverted the Truckee River, changing the landscape. Further development dug out and covered wetlands for residential and commercial buildings. The once verdant Truckee Meadows lost about half of its wetlands in the process. Oxbow Nature Study Area (Trail 17) is a recovered wetland on the northern shores of the Truckee River, where birds and other native species now thrive.

Although some trails in this section do not touch the Carson Range, the views framed within every hike prominently feature the stunning range as it climbs from its highest reaches into the high desert.

17 Oxbow Nature Study Area

DISTANCE:	0.9-mile loop
ELEVATION GAIN:	Minimal
HIGH POINT:	4560 feet
DIFFICULTY:	Easy
FITNESS:	Walkers
FAMILY-FRIENDLY:	Yes
DOG-FRIENDLY:	No
AMENITIES:	Restrooms, benches, interpretive signs
CONTACT:	City of Reno, download map from Washoe County "Truckee Meadows Trails" guide
GPS:	39.51907°, –119.84607°
BEFORE YOU GO:	Open 8 AM to sunset from June to end of October; gate is locked at 4 PM. For gate closure information, call Reno Police Department (775-334-2175).

GETTING THERE

Driving: From I-80 east, take exit 12 for Keystone Avenue. Take a right off the freeway exit to head south on Keystone. Continue for 0.5 mile, then take a right onto 2nd Street. Continue for 0.5 mile, where West 2nd turns into Dickerson. Continue straight for 0.7 mile until Dickerson dead-ends at the park.

Oxbow Nature Study Area is a 22-acre conservation area, run by a partnership between the City of Reno and the Nevada Department of Wildlife (NDOW). This area along the Truckee River features healthy wetlands and an abundance of wildlife. The mature cottonwoods, dense pockets of Russian olive and willows, and pond create an ideal environment for birds, both migrating and oversummering. A careful search for hummingbirds, herons, hawks, and thrushes can transform this twenty-minute walk into an afternoon adventure. Interpretive signs along the trail help novice wildlife spotters, as can periodic events hosted by

Expect to find wide trails under canopies of native trees at Oxbow Nature Study Area.

the Lahontan Audubon Society or NDOW (see Resources). This is a sensitive area; please obey all posted rules.

Along the drive, discover the local shops, restaurants, and artistry along Dickerson Road, one of Reno's emerging arts and culture districts. Learn more on the Visit RenoTahoe website.

GET MOVING

From the parking lot, notice two trails extending southwest, each behind a large sign. These are the two tendrils of the first loop along the trail. Start on the trail to the right (the northernmost one) to begin. Here you will see a boardwalk to the far right and a dirt path on the left. Head up the boardwalk, which leads to a vista point with a view of the rich, dense foliage as well as bits of the river and peaks of the Carson Range. Then walk down the boardwalk and continue on the dirt trail.

In about 50 feet, the trail splits again; take the right side of this fork to come to another vista point, this time a platform that extends over a pond. Here, many birds flit around the thick growth of cattails or glide across the water, all the while singing their beautiful songs. Can you hear the knocking of

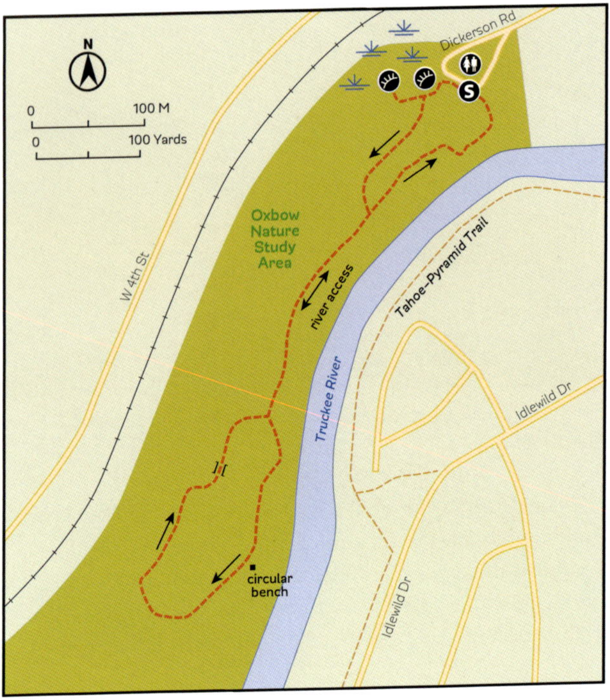

the downy woodpecker, or the rapid, tinkling *tee-yee* of the lesser goldfinch? Can you spot the slender, uniformly black figure of the double-crested cormorant, or the white-beaked American coot near the water? Take your time here, relaxing on one of the benches before returning to the trail. It is especially lovely in the morning, as there are fewer people and the birdsongs echo through the air.

Return to the main trail and continue. Here, notice the lush growth of dogbane, nightshade, yarrow, and other riparian plants. Russian olive hangs over the trail. Walk softly and you may catch sight of a rabbit or muskrat hiding within the growth. While this is an excellent place to see birds, it is also a habitat for mammals, including deer, cottontails, and beavers.

NEVADA GEOLOGY

To capture the exceptional geologic history of Nevada in this confined space is laughable. Explaining how this arid land (the driest in the country) claims sandstone as its official state rock could fill the remaining pages of this book.

There are thousands of minerals present here and a myriad of differently formed rock. Volcanic rock is prevalent, but even igneous rock is made up of different minerals like micas, hornblendes, magnesium, or calcium. Igneous rock can further be altered by hydrothermal fluids permeating layers of rock, leaving behind a catalog of unique mineral presence.

Hydrothermally altered rock is common and easily identifiable—just look toward the stunning reddish-orange-brown rock adjacent to the Hunter Creek Falls Trail (Trail 20). The rock, found standing alone on the hillsides in small formations, is indicative of hot water pushing through the quartz, crafting a harder exterior that is less prone to erosion than other rock around it. Local geologists say that careful hunting around these rocks will show little cavities (or vugs) that contain small quartz crystals.

At 0.2 mile, the trail opens up from this overgrown area to views of the Truckee River. About 75 feet later, it reaches the end of the first loop, becoming a wide path that parallels the river. Turn right here. Cottonwoods along this section add beautiful shade and color from spring to fall. At 0.3 mile, reach the second loop and take a left to follow it clockwise. Then, at 0.4 mile, notice a large circular bench and a trail to the left. There is a social trail beyond (west) of the circular bench, but it doesn't lead anywhere. Instead, make a right to stay on trail.

The trail loops around to head back north. At 0.5 mile, a trail sprouts off to the left (west); however, this is not a public trail and should not be taken. Continue northeast along the loop, slowing down because likely there will be an animal close by and you may be lucky enough to spot it.

At 0.6 mile, come to a log bridge over a creek. It should be stable, but be cautious and mindful of your step. About 300 feet later, the loop closes and deposits you back onto the wide path that parallels the Truckee River. Continue the 0.1 mile back to the first loop, but this time, take the route on your right, closest to the river. Here begins a fabulous boardwalk with a few vista points over the river. Look across and see the Idlewild to Wingfield Park section of the Tahoe-Pyramid Trail (Trail 2) wrapping around the cheery pink condos. The boardwalk brings you back to the trailhead.

18 Caughlin Ranch Path

DISTANCE:	5.4 miles roundtrip
ELEVATION GAIN:	400 feet
HIGH POINT:	4970 feet
DIFFICULTY:	Easy
FITNESS:	Walkers, runners, cyclists (no e-bikes)
FAMILY-FRIENDLY:	Yes, ADA and stroller accessible
DOG-FRIENDLY:	Yes, leashed
AMENITIES:	Pet waste stations, benches
CONTACT:	Caughlin Ranch HOA, download map from website
GPS:	39.510845°, −119.852787°
BEFORE YOU GO:	Trail is public but managed by Caughlin Ranch Homeowners Association (HOA). Respect all posted signs and private property. Do not feed birds. Keep out of ponds.

GETTING THERE

Driving: From I-80 west, take exit 10 for North McCarran Boulevard West. Turn left off the freeway exit to continue on McCarran. Continue 1.2 miles, then turn left on Mayberry Drive.

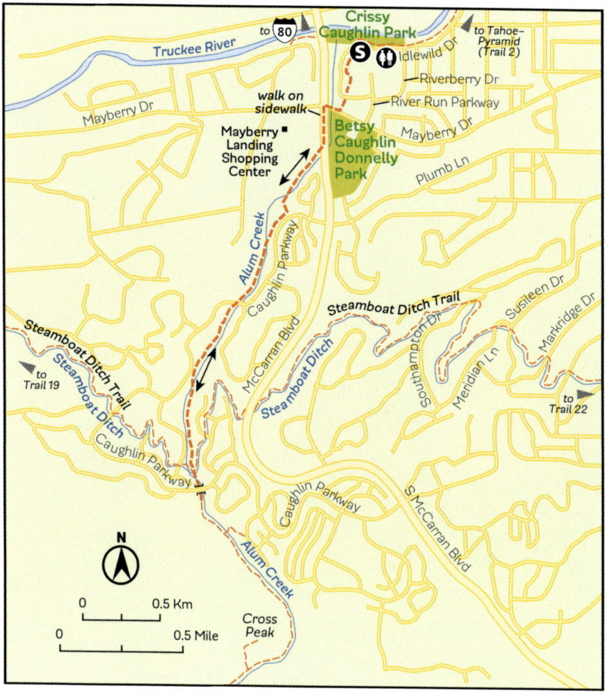

Continue for 0.2 mile, turn left on River Run Parkway, and after 0.1 mile, turn right onto Riverberry Drive. In 0.3 mile, turn left onto Idlewild Drive. Turn right into the parking lot at Crissy Caughlin Park.

While it may not offer the same rugged naturalism as other trails in this book, this trail provides a worthy experience as it follows Alum Creek to the Truckee River. It is the glass of champagne ordered on a Tuesday afternoon—glamorous and carefree. Its manicured style does not distract from the beauty of Alum Creek. Each rapid, each drop and gurgling, babbling section of the creek is highlighted against well-trimmed grass, thoughtfully placed pine trees, and ornate

Bench with a scenic view overlooking the pond along the Caughlin Ranch trail

ponds. Most importantly, it connects neighborhoods to open space so people can easily access nature. See the Go Farther section to learn how this trail extends into the Carson Range.

This trail is managed by Caughlin Ranch HOA, which generously allows public access. Don't take this privilege in vain; respect private property and posted signs, pick up after your dog, and stay on the trail. Spring and fall are beautiful times to walk this path, but it is appropriate year-round.

GET MOVING

From Crissy Caughlin Park, walk west through the park to the boundary, about 300 feet from the parking lot. The Tahoe-Pyramid Bikeway begins here. Cross the bridge and immediately look left (south) for a small dirt path that connects to the neighborhood. In about 100 feet, a paved path begins, following alongside a small creek. This is Alum Creek, and you'll be following this high desert gem the entire journey.

Follow this path for 0.4 mile, until the neighborhood ends and you reach Mayberry Drive. Turn right (west) to follow the road and pick up the trail kitty-corner from here, just north of the Mayberry Landing Shopping Center. Cross McCarran, then cross Mayberry. Don't assume right-turning traffic will see or stop for you. At the southernmost point of the shopping center (about 0.1 mile from Mayberry), a path becomes visible. This is where the Alum Creek Trail picks back up.

The trail parallels McCarran for about 0.1 mile before charging southwest along the creek. Continue for 0.3 mile before popping out along Caughlin Parkway. Here, and for the next 0.2 mile, the trail borders the southeast perimeter of a series of ponds. Weeping willow trees, fairytale footbridges, and grass made for picnics unfold, offering a dose of tranquility potent enough to forget about the surrounding neighborhood and busy roads.

At 1.6 miles, reach a confluence of trails. Continue straight (southwest), keeping Alum Creek by your side. In 0.1 mile, the trail crosses Caughlin Parkway, then moves away from the Trail, cultivating greater peace. A small trail junction appears at 1.8 miles. Continue straight.

At 2.5 miles, the Steamboat Ditch Trail (Trail 22) crosses this path on its way northwest to the Tom Cooke and Hunter Creek Trails (Trails 19 and 20). Steamboat Ditch almost looks like a social trail, a great juxtaposition to the manicured Caughlin path.

About 400 feet later, the trail wanders under a tunnel. When it pops out on the other side, the foothills start to show, and sagebrush monopolizes the environment. This shift should clue you in to looking for the end point about 0.2 mile later. The finish is not notable and nearly imperceptible, save for a bench and a transition from paved path to dirt trail. Enjoy a moment of rest at the bench, decide to hike farther (see below), or head back to Crissy Caughlin Park.

GO FARTHER

There are several easy options to extend this walk. The most obvious is to continue following Alum Creek on the dirt trail that replaces the paved path at the southern terminus. This is technically a social trail (not built or managed by Washoe County or USFS) but is on USFS land. If signs appear asking users to avoid the area, please oblige. Follow the Alum Creek Trail for another 2.1 miles and 1250 feet of elevation gain one way. This trail also gives access to climbing Cross Peak, adding 0.9 mile and 500 feet of elevation gain one way. There is private property on the west of the first 0.5 mile of trail. Be respectful here.

Steamboat Ditch (Trail 22) is another great option, as this 18-mile trail (if you follow it in its entirety) provides ample discoveries. Take it in either direction for beautiful views.

19 Tom Cooke Loop

DISTANCE:	3.8-mile loop
ELEVATION GAIN:	400 feet
HIGH POINT:	4930 feet
DIFFICULTY:	Moderate to challenging
FITNESS:	Walkers, hikers, runners, cyclists
FAMILY-FRIENDLY:	Yes, keep young children close around cyclists.
DOG-FRIENDLY:	Yes, leashed
AMENITIES:	Pet waste station, benches, portable restrooms, barbecue and picnic areas
CONTACT:	City of Reno, download map from website
GPS:	39.505306°, -119.902194°
BEFORE YOU GO:	Rattlesnakes sighted in area

GETTING THERE

Driving: From downtown Reno, head west on West 4th Street for 4.8 miles. At the roundabout, take the second exit onto

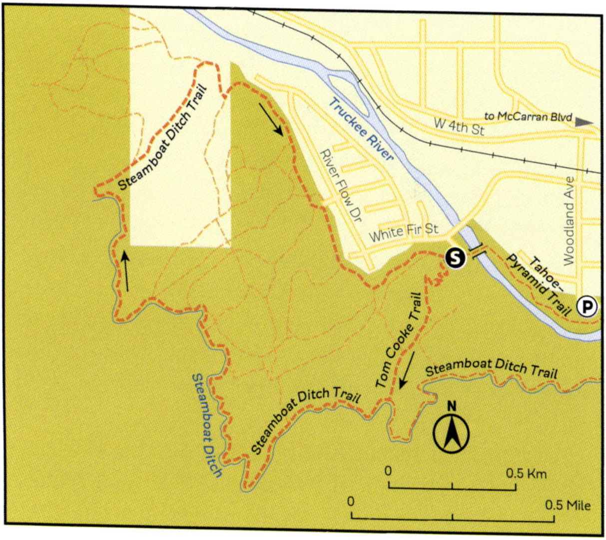

Woodland Avenue. Continue over the train tracks, then make the first right onto White Fir Street. Continue for 0.4 mile. Just after you pass the river, turn left into the trailhead parking lot. Note: Additional parking can be found at Mayberry Park. To access it, follow Woodland Avenue about 0.4 mile until it dead-ends at the park.

Popular with cyclists, the Tom Cooke Trail connects the Truckee River with the golden foothills above. Though technically only half a mile one-way, it provides access to a world of exploration. Note that this trail's difficulty is listed as moderate to challenging because of the steep approach and tricky navigation. The loop described below combines Tom Cooke with the Steamboat Ditch Trail (Trail 22) and several Forest Service trails. It is a great introduction to the area and can be used as a guide for future adventures.

Like many of the open spaces surrounding Reno, trails at these Mayberry foothills create a labyrinth. While this can be delightful if time is not an issue, bring a map to orient yourself among the many trail crossings. Though the initial climb is exposed, the trail along the Steamboat Ditch can be lovely year-round. Plan to visit in the morning or evening during summer, or any time of day October–May.

GET MOVING

Locate the trail at the southeastern side of the parking lot— it starts with eight switchbacks. This section is the steepest and most challenging of the hike. Pace yourself here to ascend more than 200 feet in 0.3 mile. Several social trails cut these switchbacks. Though it may be painful, please stick to the main trail.

The top of this heart-thumper opens up to the wild space of the foothills. Here, many trails spiral off, but stay on the main trail. Two hundred feet after you've reached the top of the switchbacks, continue straight to stay on the Tom Cooke Trail.

Sunflowers and lush greenery appear along the trail in summer.

In front of you are the mountains that tower over Hunter Creek Falls (Trail 20) and the expanse of land that the Hunter Foothill Road rests on.

At 0.6 mile, after the second incline of 50 feet, reach the Steamboat Ditch Trail. Make a right and follow it along the water. Steamboat Ditch is a canal built in 1880 to divert water from the Truckee River to alfalfa farms in south Reno. Its 18-mile path (if you follow entire trail) has long since been used as by hikers and cyclists (see Steamboat Ditch, Trail 22).

Along the ditch, gorgeous plants grow. Chokecherry bushes provide some cover, though the trail is still pretty exposed. A

The hillside near Steamboat Ditch is dotted with green.

surprising number of flowers thrive here; look for paintbrush, mariposa lily, prickly poppy, arrowleaf balsamroot, lupine, and showy milkweed.

At 1.6 miles, a smaller trail branches off toward the right. Continue straight but keep a sharp eye because in just 0.2 mile, another enticing trail splits off to the right. Keep straight here too. At 1.9 miles, the trail forks; keep left. Enjoy this brief verdant section. At 2 miles, cross a small stream and continue along the trail.

At 2.4 miles, the popular Hole-in-the-Wall feature appears. It is a tunnel blasted through the rock face to create access for the flow of the Steamboat Ditch. A partial fence and no trespassing sign block folks from exploring this tunnel; please stay on the trail and out of the water. Ignore the well-defined trail that continues to the west and up a steep hill, and instead make a sharp right, followed by another sharp right (a U-turn). Enjoy wild sunflowers in this area in summer.

Almost immediately (in 0.1 mile) a smaller, skinny trail pops off to the left, making a steep ascent. Ignore this and take the easier, flatter, and wider trail that continues straight. The trail does become rocky here; be mindful of your step.

At 2.8 miles, the trail dead-ends into an east-west trail. Continue right to walk eastbound on this trail. Cross the stream 0.1 mile later, then immediately turn right on a smaller trail. There is a posted sign to direct hikers here. If you miss this and continue straight, however, you'll quickly realize your mistake, as the trail stops in 100 feet.

The trail parallels the neighborhood from this point on. There are a variety of social trails, leading from the neighborhood to the hills. A good rule in this section is to stick to the trail that parallels closest to the neighborhood. Continue for the next 0.9 mile until the trail completes the loop.

GO FARTHER

The Tom Cooke Trail neighbors major trails, making this a pleasant spot to jump into more adventures. The Idlewild to Wingfield Park Trail (Trail 2) can be located by crossing the footbridge over the Truckee River and making a right toward Mayberry Park. Here, cool off under beautiful cottonwoods and with ample river access points. From the bridge to the end of Mayberry Park is about 3700 feet.

Another option is to explore Steamboat Ditch (Trail 22) by heading east along the canal when the Tom Cooke Trail dead-ends into it. In 1.6 miles, the trail connects to Hunter Creek Falls (Trail 20), another fabulous area to explore.

20 Hunter Creek Falls Trail

DISTANCE:	6.2 miles roundtrip
ELEVATION GAIN:	1180 feet
HIGH POINT:	6130 feet
DIFFICULTY:	Moderate
FITNESS:	Walker, hikers, runners
FAMILY-FRIENDLY:	Yes, but beware of rocky sections, steep drop-offs, narrow trail, little shade
DOG-FRIENDLY:	Yes, leashed for first mile only
AMENITIES:	Pet waste stations, picnic benches, seasonal restrooms
CONTACT:	Washoe County, download map from website
GPS:	39.492794°, -119.894777°
BEFORE YOU GO:	Spikes or other traction devices for shoes advisable during winter; sections with very steep drop-offs, very rocky sections, and narrow trail

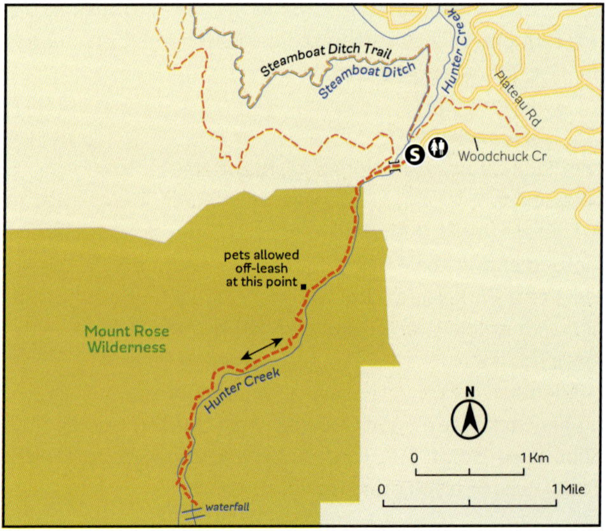

GETTING THERE

Driving: From I-80 west, take exit 10 for North McCarran Boulevard. Continue south on McCarran for 1.2 miles. Turn left at Mayberry Drive and continue for 1.3 miles. Take a left on Plateau Road and continue for 1.1 miles. Then turn right on Woodchuck Circle and continue for 0.8 mile. When you get to the roundabout, take the first exit and follow the road to the bottom parking lot. Parking during the weekend can be challenging.

Hunter Creek Falls Trail is one of the most popular in the area, perhaps because it features the only waterfall in Reno. It travels into the northeastern tip of Mount Rose Wilderness, a 30,000-acre area that takes its name from the highest peak in Washoe County. Please note that bicycles are prohibited in the Mount Rose Wilderness.

The 30-foot Hunter Creek Falls is robust year-round, with the creek adding beautiful audio along the beginning and end of the trail. While the trail is exposed for the majority of the climb, the last mile offers a cool respite from a hot summer's day. Surrounded by pines and decorated with creeks, it transforms the high desert into an oasis.

This trail is busiest during spring, when the waterfall is at its fullest. During this time, parking can be very challenging. Try for a later start time, like a couple of hours before dusk. During the winter, snow is likely along the last couple of miles.

GET MOVING

Locate the dirt trail on the western side of the parking lot. Here it is wide and soft, accented by the occasional dog poop. This is a not-so-gentle reminder of why picking up after your pup is important. Continue for 0.1 mile. A trail appears on the right (north) side of the trail and switches back to travel east. This is a connection trail for the Steamboat Ditch Trail. Maps at the trailhead describe access to the Steamboat Ditch on both sides of Hunter Creek; however, this trail is the safest option. See Go Farther to learn more.

Looking west from this trail junction, a trail split wraps around Hunter Creek. To the right is creek access and a crossing point for horses. Keep straight to walk over the bridge. Pause here to enjoy views of the rushing creek heading toward the greater Reno area.

A junction appears about 0.2 mile past the bridge. Here, a trail switches back east, connecting to Belli Front Road. When the Hunter Creek Trail is super busy, this is a great alternative (see Go Farther). In 100 feet, a smaller trail splits off to the right, part of a network of social trails. There are also several that meet with the creek. Ignore all such trails; they are not maintained and may be unsafe, and they also erode the hills and creek banks and invade homes of little critters. Stick to the established trails.

At 0.4 mile, the trail crosses into the Mount Rose Wilderness and moves away from the creek floor. You may want to look away from the growing drop-off on the creek side of the trail. The way is narrow here, and passing traffic can be difficult to maneuver at times. Trail etiquette gives uphill traffic the right of way, but here, do whatever makes the safest sense.

By 0.6 mile, you've gained 250 feet of elevation. Only 930 more feet to climb! Expect a steady grade of 250 feet every 0.6 to 0.8 mile. Because the trail is exposed, the grade can become taxing. Pace yourself, using breaks as an excuse to marvel at the variety of incredible plants in the high desert. You may spot Brown's peony, mariposa lily, western columbine, or snowplant.

At 0.8 mile, boulders take over the trail's dirt tread, forcing hikers to climb over. While the path over them should be stable, test each rock before entrusting it to bear your weight. The trail features rocky sections like this on and off for the next 0.2 mile. Rattlesnakes do love rocks, and while our Great Basin rattlesnake will move away from places of heavy traffic, it is wise

Hunter Creek Falls is Reno's only waterfall and a year-round spectacle.

to watch pets and children closely—no poking noses or hands in mystery rock crevasses. Note that pets may be unleashed after the first mile of trail; this milestone is marked with a sign.

At 1.2 miles, the trail passes under pines as it gains another 250 feet. This foliage is just a taste of the forest that awaits.

Look off toward Hunter Creek for the next three-quarters of a mile or so, especially during the fall, at the aspens creating a shimmering, stunning scene. Another benefit of a late afternoon stroll is that at 1.9 miles, shade envelops the trail as it curves south beneath a mountain.

THE VITAL TRUCKEE RIVER

For thousands of years, the Indigenous peoples in the area survived off the Truckee River's waters and habitats. In the 1860s, Alexis Waldemar Von Schmidt, a civil engineer, wanted to reroute the Truckee River to San Francisco to supply drinking water for residents. However, the prosperous soil of the Truckee Meadows, paired with the Virginia City gold discovery and Central Pacific Railroad development, meant ranchers and farmers were already settling within the Truckee's reaches. Von Schmidt's plan was overrun, and the river remained eastbound, feeding the Truckee Meadows.

Called Welganuk by the Washoe people, the Truckee Meadows area is roughly defined by the Carson Range to the west, Peavine Mountain to the north, the Virginia Range to the east, and Steamboat Hills to the south. Before agriculture and development, it was an "emerald-green valley covered over by tules and ryegrass," wrote John M. Townley, describing immigrants' opinions in his series *Tough Little Town on the Truckee.*

Lush and fertile as the meadows once were, the Truckee River is a symbol of the Great Basin; its waters never reach the ocean, instead remaining at Pyramid Lake. It is one of the few waterways that shelter Lahontan cutthroat trout, a threatened species that once swam in the great Lahontan lake that spanned much of northern Nevada, as well as parts of southern Oregon and eastern California.

While the river still flows, a series of diversion ditches (like Steamboat Ditch, Trail 22) and development have reduced its might. Today, it supplies about 80 percent of the region's drinking water and serves as a rich recreation site for fishing, birding, swimming and water sports, and hiking. Thanks to the Tahoe-Pyramid Trail, we can enjoy 114 miles of its shoreline. From drinking water to recreation to incredible biodiversity of the associated wetlands, the Truckee Meadows is a vibrant representation of the life water brings to the desert.

Cross the first of three creeks at 2.5 miles. This one is small and shallow; there might not be a creek here at all in dry years. There are usually rocks you can use to cross, but be careful: it's always better to have a soggy shoe than a twisted ankle nearly 3 miles from the car. From here, the trail gains 70 quick feet in 0.1 mile, but the bordering brooks and gentle spires of fir and pine soothe any uphill pain.

At 2.6 miles, cross another creek, this one slightly larger but manageable. Still, take caution. The trail slithers through trees, depositing hikers at a slightly confusing area about 220 feet before the trail ends. You will want to cross Hunter Creek; there is a lovely spot to sit on the other side, with a fantastic view of the waterfall. A social trail attempting to cross here looks as established (maybe even more so) than the actual trail, which continues for another 70 feet before crossing. Water levels dictate safe crossings; take whatever feels best to you.

When you've had your fill, follow the same trail back to the trailhead, remembering to leash dogs again about a mile from the trailhead.

GO FARTHER

Add more miles by exploring the mountains bordering the north side of the Hunter Creek Falls Trail. Begin at the same trailhead and follow directions to 0.2 mile. Here, take the trail on the right, heading up the mountain. Belli Front Road adds 4.7 miles and 800 feet of elevation. Enjoy wildflowers and views of the city and Verdi.

You could also connect to the Steamboat Ditch Trail (Trail 22). Locate the trail junction at 0.1 mile, then turn left (if coming from the falls) and continue along the creek. The trail dead-ends at a metal bridge over Steamboat Ditch; Hunter Creek is about 15 feet below. Carefully hop up along the side of the ditch to cross. Then take the Steamboat Ditch Trail north to the Tom Cooke (Trail 19) area or south through Caughlin Ranch, under South McCarran Boulevard to Horseman's Sports Park.

21 Cold Canyon Loop

DISTANCE: 3.8-mile loop
ELEVATION GAIN: 760 feet
HIGH POINT: 5880 feet
DIFFICULTY: Moderate
FITNESS: Walkers, hikers, runners, cyclists
FAMILY-FRIENDLY: Yes
DOG-FRIENDLY: Yes, leashed
AMENITIES: None
CONTACT: US Forest Service and other agencies
GPS: 39.4754846°, −119.8541622°
BEFORE YOU GO: Trails are shared with OHV users. Expect to see motorized users while hiking here.

GETTING THERE

Driving: From South McCarran Boulevard, turn onto Caughlin Parkway. Continue for 0.2 mile, then turn left onto Village Green Parkway. In 0.5 mile, turn left onto Pinehaven Road and

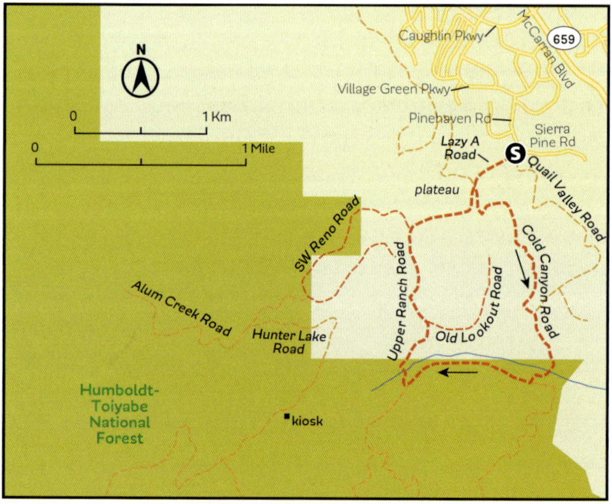

go 0.3 mile to the dead end. Park along the street, but don't block vehicle access to the dirt roads.

This route combines several off-highway vehicle (OHV) trails to create a loop along beautiful vistas and into a verdant creek valley. Though this route uses OHV trails, it is very popular with hikers and mountain bikers. For the most part, vehicles only drive along the western side of the loop (and generally only for the last mile). Dog walkers and those with young children should be cautious but also feel absolutely comfortable using this trail. Spring and fall are gorgeous times to catch the foliage along the creek, but dry winter days are magical too.

GET MOVING

From Pinehaven Road, look south into the open space. There will be obvious trails paralleling themselves, heading southwest; they land in the same place, with a nominal difference in elevation or distance. Take the one that suits your mood. The beginning of this route may be a bit confusing, but it gets easier as the trail shakes out.

In the first 400 feet, these trails feel like they splinter into dozens more. Many meet back up with each other, so maintain a southwesterly direction. The true marker indicating you are going the right way is the large plateau (the Lazy A Plateau), about 0.2 mile and 120 feet of elevation up from the trailhead. It is common to see cars (and, unfortunately, trash) here. There is a smaller plateau carved out on the north side of these trails. This is the wrong one. You do not need to make any sharp turns.

At this plateau, look south and locate the easternmost trail that hugs the mountainside and appears to be level. Take this and leave the congested area.

As the trail curves around the mountain, a world of wild plants replaces the bald dirt of the OHV tracks. Tall grasses sway in the springtime wind, curl leaf mountain mahogany grows as tall as trees, and western wallflowers glow yellow. In the distance, scattered pine trees await.

At 1.1 miles, a trail goes right, though it doesn't look as convincing as your current path. Ignore it and continue southeast for 260 feet, where multiple trails fan out. One heads northeast, another directly east, and another south. Take the trail leading south (on the right) and continue for 0.5 mile.

At 1.6 miles, the trail descends to a creek. Depending on the time of year and the force of that year's winter, it may require careful rock-hopping to cross. Remember: it is always better to get your feet wet walking through a creek than to twist an ankle trying to hop over. After reaching the opposite bank, the trail heads briefly east before switching back west to parallel the creek. Another trail does extend east instead of switching back here. If you take it by mistake, you will be stopped by a fence in about 500 feet.

Heading west, keeping the creek on your right (north), notice how overgrown and lush this creek canyon is. The mountainside lining the left (south) of the trail has extensive new pine growth—rows and rows and rows of trees 3–5 feet tall, watched over by their mature parents farther up the hill. Along the creek, aspen and sunflower grow. Especially May–June, the most notable thing growing is the antelope bitterbrush, leaning over the trail with the weight of its bright yellow flowers.

At 2.2 miles, the trail veers to the right, then makes a sharp right to approach the creek. This crossing is more challenging than the first, as the creek creates a pool here. Watch your footing. Continue straight from the creek crossing for another 400 feet. Sorry to say, but here, the tranquil stroll along the creek is interrupted by a 200-foot climb up an exposed, desiccated hill. At 2.4 miles, look to the right (east). Here, notice a remnant of Reno past: a rusted-out car that nature is attempting to recruit. Other cars like this are hidden around

Hiking along the eastern side of Cold Canyon Loop

local trails, and such secret relics are more fun to happen upon than have pointed out.

As the climb eases, around 2.8 miles, the environment again opens up. Trails scatter across this area, creating a complex intersection. You might be inclined to continue straight along the trail that wraps around the hillside. However, keep to the trails on the right (east), and choose anything that heads directly north with a slight decrease in elevation.

About 0.3 mile from this intersection, the trails dead-end into ones traveling east–west. Turn right to head east, following the trail back to the great plateau at Lazy A Road. The trailhead should be visible along this last stretch, showing the correct way down.

Looking east toward downtown Reno from the Cold Canyon Loop

GO FARTHER

An easy, gorgeous way to extend this hike is to take the 0.5-mile Old Lookout Road that splits east from the Cold Canyon Loop at 2.6 miles. In total, this extension adds around 200 feet of elevation gain as it travels the mile out and back from the main loop. The vista is a beautiful look down onto Reno, from the university to South Meadows.

The Hunter Lake Road and Southwest Reno Road loop offers another option, adding 1.6 miles and 300 feet of elevation gain. It breaks off to the west at 3 miles, before the Cold Canyon Trail turns back to the east.

22 Steamboat Ditch Trail

DISTANCE:	3.1 miles roundtrip
ELEVATION GAIN:	Minimal
HIGH POINT:	4920 feet
DIFFICULTY:	Easy
FITNESS:	Walkers, runners, cyclists
FAMILY-FRIENDLY:	Yes
DOG-FRIENDLY:	Yes, leashed
AMENITIES:	Pet waste stations, benches
CONTACT:	Steamboat Canal and Irrigation Company
GPS:	39.48313°, -119.83293°
BEFORE YOU GO:	Trail approaches private property and at times even crosses it; please be respectful

GETTING THERE

Driving: From NV 659 (South McCarran Boulevard) in either direction, turn onto Skyline Boulevard where it makes a T intersection with McCarran and continue for 0.8 mile. Turn right onto Pioneer Drive and continue for 120 feet before turning right into the Horseman's Park parking lot.

One of the longest in the area, the Steamboat Ditch Trail provides access to open space from numerous neighborhoods. Because it does not demand a lot from users, it is great for days when you need a dependable trail to let your mind relax. Note that it is a very busy trail and popular with dog walkers.

Though beloved and widely used for decades, the Steamboat Ditch is technically a social trail on private land. The trail featured here is an access road for the Steamboat Canal and Irrigation Company (SCIC), which owns an easement to the ditch. There has been controversy about closing this trail (see "The History of Steamboat Ditch" sidebar). While it remains open to the public at the time of writing, that privilege may be revoked. Follow all posted signs and regulations. Do not cross private property lines. Be respectful of SCIC's vehicles or employees. Leash pets and keep them away from private residences. With respectful collaboration, we can hopefully continue to enjoy this route for years to come.

GET MOVING

There is no wrong way to enjoy this trail. Extending 18 miles from within the McCarran loop to Verdi, this trail touches countless neighborhoods and connects urban areas with open space. For those new to the trail, this section is an introduction to the most easily accessed trailhead at Horseman's Park. See Go Farther for information about the trail.

Locate the trailhead at the west side of the parking lot. It is marked by a trail sign that says Pedestrian Crossing Only and a wide dirt path with intermittent wooden steps. Turn right on the first dirt path that leads north. When walking westward, the Steamboat Ditch is always on the left of the trail for the full 18-mile journey. Soon the trail crosses Skyline Boulevard. Continue straight across the street. It will look like you are entering someone's driveway, but the dirt path soon resumes as you head west. This is not the only time the trail comes close to homes or crosses what looks like a private drive.

At 0.2 mile, views open up before the trail turns and heads northwest. Notice the stately cottonwood trees, a sign that water is nearby. Various other creeks and washes cross the ditch along its journey, at times creating a sandwich of green. At 0.3 mile, the trail opens up to the east, revealing views of the Reno skyline. This is a taste of what this trail offers: a tunnel vision view of the city's most iconic buildings and views.

At 0.4 mile, the trail comes to its second street crossing (there are a total of four). The next 0.4 mile heads west, where willowy plants line the trail, creating an overgrown green garden from spring to late summer, with the Carson Range peeking through. Around 0.7 mile, as the trail marches east again, views sweep the Virginia Range. At 1 mile, the trail comes again to a road crossing. This time, the road is marked with a white fence

Bright greenery along Steamboat Ditch

on both sides of the street. There is no crosswalk here, and the road curves, so be cautious. This crossing is a bit confusing, but remember to keep the ditch to your left.

The trail continues straight (northwest) for another 0.1 mile before curving to the right. Here, at this trail direction change, lies a dry valley with grasses and sparse trees. Though there is little shade for the rest of the trail, this limited foliage leads to more great views of the city and Virginia Range, as well as the Carson Range on the way back.

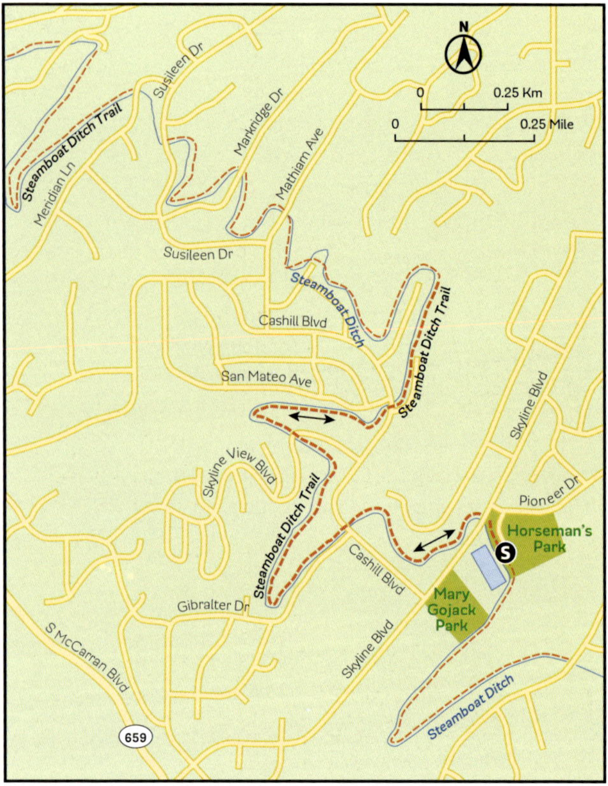

Cross the last road at 1.4 miles. This is an easy one to navigate. Notice that there is a pet waste station, one of only a few along the trail. The last 0.2 mile opens up as it steers away from the neighborhood, a great finale before heading back to Horseman's Park.

GO FARTHER

From Horseman's Park, the Steamboat Ditch travels to the hillside above Mayberry Park—see Trail 19, the Tom Cooke Loop. It crosses Alum Creek (see Caughlin Ranch Path,

Trail 18) and Hunter Creek (Trail 20) along the way, traveling through a tunnel under South McCarran Boulevard. In addition to Horseman's Park, along Woodchuck Circle (about a mile east of the Hunter Creek Falls Trail), there are two more great access points: Mayberry Park and the Tom Cooke trailhead parking lot.

If you continue northwest on the trail, at 2.3 miles it will eventually require you to walk down a private residence's driveway to Southampton Road. The homeowners welcome trail users and have posted signs clarifying this. Another lovely way to extend your time is to return to Horseman's Park and continue southeast for 1.2 miles (one-way). At the park, walk south past the parking lot and turn right when the hillside drops away. This section ducks down to a lovely stream crossing with lush riparian plants and, though it is lined with neighborhoods, provides a wide-open view both east and west.

THE HISTORY OF STEAMBOAT DITCH

This trail is represented here because public access was widely publicized during a 2021 controversy. The SCIC wished to make improvements on the canal that would have closed access to the trail. Public outcry, which according to the *Reno Gazette Journal* consisted of "roughly 1,500 emails and 150 voicemails regarding the project, as well as a handful of letters"—halted plans and kept this route open . . . at least for now.

Patricia Andrew notes in a research paper about the area, "But one gets the feeling that the Steamboat Ditch . . . will always be the center of controversy." The 2021 outcry was not a singular event. Over the years, other residential areas along the canal lines have sparked conflict. Local lore recounts landowners trying everything they can to keep the public away from their property. They have built gates, which the public would then climb. Guards were hired, but crafty users got around them. One landowner went so far as to put axle grease on her gates to dissuade climbers, which a local cleaned off with WD-40 and a rag. Through the tumultuous (and perhaps exaggerated) history, one thing is clear: the Steamboat Ditch is an important trail to Renoites.

23 Virginia Lake Loop

DISTANCE:	1-mile loop
ELEVATION GAIN:	Minimal
HIGH POINT:	4490 feet
DIFFICULTY:	Easy
FITNESS:	Walkers, runners
FAMILY-FRIENDLY:	Yes, ADA and stroller accessible
DOG-FRIENDLY:	Yes, leashed; see map for off-leash area
AMENITIES:	Benches, restrooms, barbecue grills, interpretive signs, water fountain, off-leash dog park, exercise equipment, picnic shelter, playground, fishing pier
CONTACT:	City of Reno, download map from website
GPS:	39.503584°, -119.806609°
BEFORE YOU GO:	Open 5 AM–10 PM April 1–September 30 and 6 AM–7 PM October 1–March 31

GETTING THERE

Public Transit: Take RTC 6 to the Brinkby Avenue and Lakeside Drive stop. From here, walk two blocks north to access the lake. Your walk begins at the south end of the lake.

Driving: From the intersection of Plumb Lane and South Virginia Street in Reno, travel west on Plumb for 0.2 mile. Make the first left onto Lakeside Drive. In 0.1 mile, continue straight onto Lymbery Street. In 200 feet, park in the small lot on the right. Additional curbside parking is available around the lake.

Virginia Lake welcomes those seeking a quick escape and dose of nature within the otherwise crowded streets of shopping malls, casinos, and traffic. Initially created as a fishing lake, it is still a fantastic place to cast. The Nevada Department of Wildlife (NDOW) stocks the lake with rainbow trout and other species. In fact, an angler caught the state's record carp here in 2020. Contact NDOW to obtain a fishing license (see Resources). The lake is not just great for fishing; native

This dragonfly sculpture at Virginia Lake was made by local artist Peter Hazel from steel, glass, and recycled ceramics. Look for it near the nature trails at the southern end of the lake.

plants and a variety of waterfowl make it a gorgeous, relaxing place to enjoy the Nevada sunshine.

Some trail reviews call Virginia Lake an urban oasis; others say it is "dirty, nasty, crowded, and scary." Regardless of time of day or year, it is a very popular trail. The only thing that might cause distress are the flocks of habituated geese, ducks, and pigeons that people are warned against feeding. If you protect your lunch and your dog doesn't approach a parenting goose, you should have no problem relaxing.

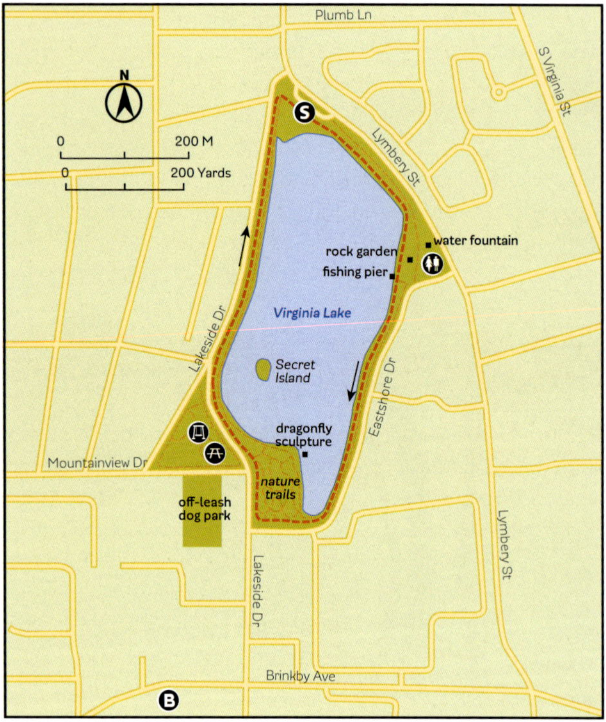

GET MOVING

Either direction in which you walk around the lake (clockwise or counterclockwise) is fine. The only difference is that clockwise users may get better views of Mount Rose for a longer period of time. For this reason, directions here follow this route.

From the parking lot, start walking east, on a section of trail lined with junipers. Also notice a sand path in addition to the paved one. Posted signs ask slower traffic to walk on the right, along the sandy path.

At 0.1 mile, the trail begins to curve to the south. Here, find the year-round restroom and water fountain to the left.

Just south of this, notice a water feature cascading over tiers of rock. Benches and seats carved from rock, almost like a giant abalone shell, surround this decorative fountain. In summer, the soft purple flowers of Russian sage offset the gray-and-tan rock. On the other side (west) of this feature is a rock garden, with a small labyrinth of red rock–lined trails that squiggle around tall cactus and sage. Notice the buddha figure carved into stone within the first 200 feet of the garden, begging walkers to enjoy a moment of tranquility.

Back on the main trail, continue south and find the fishing pier, 50 feet from the rock garden, extending over the lake. One reason to visit the dock, beyond casual fishing, is to watch the variety of birds on the lake. American coots, black-crowned night herons, common mergansers, and variety of grebes can be found in plenty here.

Continue south for another 0.2 mile to the southern end of the lake. The dragonfly sculpture, set above the water, comes into view here. Get a better view of this artwork (originally presented at Burning Man, but later dedicated to the park by the artist) as the trail loops around and meets with the nature trails. To reach them, stay right on the sand path as it diverts from the paved path.

This 0.1-mile extension through the nature trails is another great place to look for birds congregating on the island and along the rocky shore. Spot flocks of California gulls and double-crested cormorants as the small trail loops around native plants to the lake's shoreline. Be warned—groups of pigeons and geese congregate here. Make a full loop of the nature trails, then return to their split from the paved path. Continue west, making a northbound turn when the trail approaches Lakeside Drive. About 100 feet later, find the playground, picnic shelters, and off-leash dog park across Lakeside Drive. Continue straight. At 0.9 mile, turn right and cross the bridge to come back into the parking lot.

24 Bartley Ranch Regional Park

DISTANCE:	Up to 2.1 miles of trails
ELEVATION GAIN:	Up to 370 feet
HIGH POINT:	4700 feet
DIFFICULTY:	Easy to moderate
FITNESS:	Walkers, runners, hikers, cyclists (prohibited on Flume and Quail Run Trails)
FAMILY-FRIENDLY:	Yes
DOG-FRIENDLY:	Yes, leashed
AMENITIES:	Pet waste stations, benches, picnic areas, restrooms, interpretive center, cultural displays
CONTACT:	Washoe County, download map from website
GPS:	39.469781°, -119.8073539°
BEFORE YOU GO:	Open sunrise to sunset (hours posted at entry gate). Park borders private property, and farm animals may be present. Be respectful; keep pets and children close.

GETTING THERE

Driving: From I-580 south (US Highway 395 south), take exit 31 for South Kietzke Lane. Take a left off the freeway exit and continue on Kietzke for 0.1 mile, then turn right on McCarran Boulevard. After 0.8 mile, turn left onto Lakeside Drive. Continue for 0.4 mile, then turn left onto Bartley Ranch Road and continue 200 feet across the bridge. After you cross the bridge, turn right into the parking lot by the historic school.

Bartley Ranch Regional Park offers a great combination of amenities for people looking for history, nature, and Reno charm. The land sits on the historical Wheeler Estate, used for farming, ranching, and horse training until 1985. Within the 117 acres is a pasture, equestrian arena, Robert Z. Hawkins amphitheater (see Washoe County website for events), interpretive

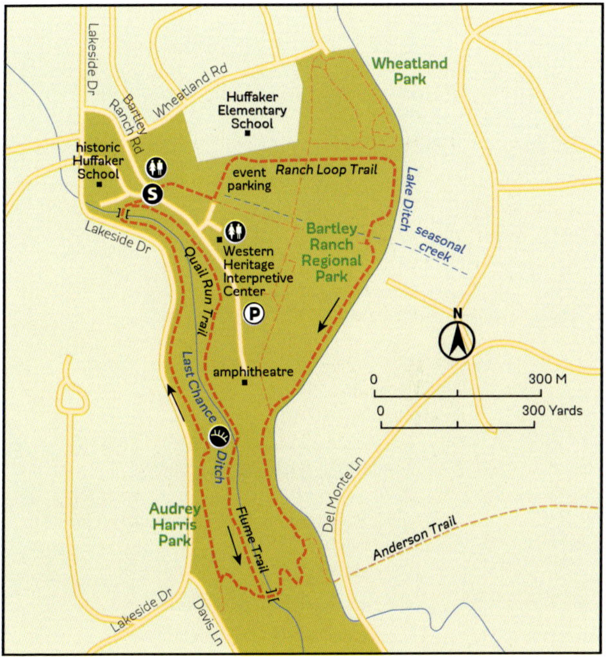

center, the restored historical Huffaker School, and three trails. Hikers and cyclists must yield to equestrians. Last Chance Ditch and Lake Ditch run along the trails, creating vibrant habitat for vegetation and wildlife. The farming equipment and interpretive center offer great interactive features for children (and adults) to enjoy while taking in a dose of a classic Nevada landscape.

Last Chance Ditch and Lake Ditch divert from the Truckee River and are part of the many historical ditches used for agriculture in the late nineteenth to early twentieth centuries. Though alfalfa crops have gone out of fashion, both ditches are still in use today. Learn more about this history on the Steamboat Ditch Trail (see sidebar in Trail 22).

Remnants of the park's past life as a working ranch and farm, as seen from Quail Run Trail near the Western Heritage Interpretive Center

GET MOVING

Locate the trail to the left (east) of the restrooms. There will be a sign for Ranch Loop Trail and Quail Run Trail. The route described here goes clockwise around the Ranch Loop Trail, meeting back up at this trailhead to take the Quail Run and Flume Trails.

Take the leftmost trail, which crosses Bartley Ranch Road and then snakes between a picnic pavilion and a creek. About 280 feet from the road crossing, reach a parking lot. Walk to the end of the lot, then turn left to cross the bridge, where the trail drops into an overfill event parking lot. This section can feel like you've gotten lost completely, but stick with it. Head directly northeast across the parking lot to where the Great

Basin sagebrush fills in again, about 300 feet. At the Ranch Loop sign, turn right to continue east.

Take in views of the Virginia Range and pass Huffaker Elementary School on the north side of the trail. Immediately after the school is Wheatland Park on the left, with paved trails and access to the neighborhood. Continue straight to stay on the Ranch Loop Trail. A wooden corral appears on the right, along with a beautiful view of Slide Mountain. At 0.4 mile, the antique farm equipment displays begin, dotting every 150 feet or so of the trail, each with a sign explaining how the equipment works and its purpose.

The trail sweeps around to the south and, about 0.1 mile from the first farming display, reaches the creek again. This is easy to miss, as this northern side of the creek isn't marked and another trail continues west. Cross the creek, then turn left to stay on the Ranch Loop. For the next 0.2 mile, continue straight, keeping Lake Ditch on your left. The occasional trail spurs off northwest or east across the ditch—ignore these.

At 0.7 mile, Ranch Loop Trail dead-ends. Turn left here to continue south, where the trail transforms, becoming smaller and rockier. The Lake Ditch follows along like a faithful companion as you travel the next 0.2 mile, where the trail splits again. To the left is the start of the Anderson Trail (see Go Farther). Keep right to head southwest.

In the next 0.1 mile, the trail switches back twice. It looks like a lot of elevation to gain, but don't worry: less than 100 feet of gain awaits over the next 0.4 mile. Cross Last Chance Ditch and immediately after, note the Flume Trail connection on the right. For now, continue straight for another 0.1 mile, where the trail dead-ends again near Lakeside Drive. Turn right and head north, then arrive in Audrey Harris Park, marking the end of its uphill journey. Pause to take in the sweeping view and Reno landmarks, then exit on the north side of the parking lot. The trail parallels Lakeside Drive for the next 0.3 mile as it gradually loses elevation. At 1.5 miles, turn right, cross Last Chance Ditch again, and find yourself back at the trailhead; equestrians and cyclists must end their adventure here.

To explore the park's other two trails, turn right at a well-marked junction to head southeast on the Quail Run Nature Trail. Quail Run, along with the Flume Trail, only allows foot traffic.

The Quail Run Trail starts in a corridor of tall shrubs, including golden current, which flowers yellow in early spring. Soon, cross a small wooden footbridge to head even deeper into this serene area. The quietness erases the proximity of Lakeside and the greater Reno metropolis as quail, kinglets, jays, chickadees, and magpies flit from shrub to shrub. After 400 feet, the environment begins to open up, revealing cottonwoods, pines, and lovely benches to sit and rest. A short distance farther, find the Western Heritage Interpretive Center.

Continue on as Quail Run shifts into the Flume Trail along Last Chance Ditch, adjacent to the amphitheater. The flume is characterized by wood planks that look like train tracks. Continue along this wooden path. At 0.4 mile, Last Chance Ditch diverts from the trail, which becomes a sneaky little thing, shying away to the right and turning back to dirt. Follow it for 0.2 mile, until it meets back at the Last Chance Ditch bridge and Ranch Loop. Either turn around to take the Flume and Quail Trails back to the parking lot, or turn right (west) and retrace your steps on the Ranch Loop back to the lot.

GO FARTHER

The Anderson Trail adds 1.7 miles roundtrip and connects Bartley Ranch Regional Park with Anderson Park. It passes pastures, and seeing cattle is a regular occurrence. To access it, turn right (east) at the Ranch Loop's 0.9-mile mark. The trail will switch back, then cross Del Monte Lane.

25 Ballardini Ranch Loop

DISTANCE:	2.2-mile loop
ELEVATION GAIN:	280 feet
HIGH POINT:	5060 feet
DIFFICULTY:	Easy to moderate
FITNESS:	Walkers, hikers, runners, cyclists
FAMILY-FRIENDLY:	Yes
DOG-FRIENDLY:	Yes, leashed
AMENITIES:	Pet waste stations, trash cans, pit toilet, covered picnic area
CONTACT:	Washoe County, download map from website
GPS:	39.44751°, -119.82194°
BEFORE YOU GO:	Open sunrise to sunset (hours posted at entry gate)

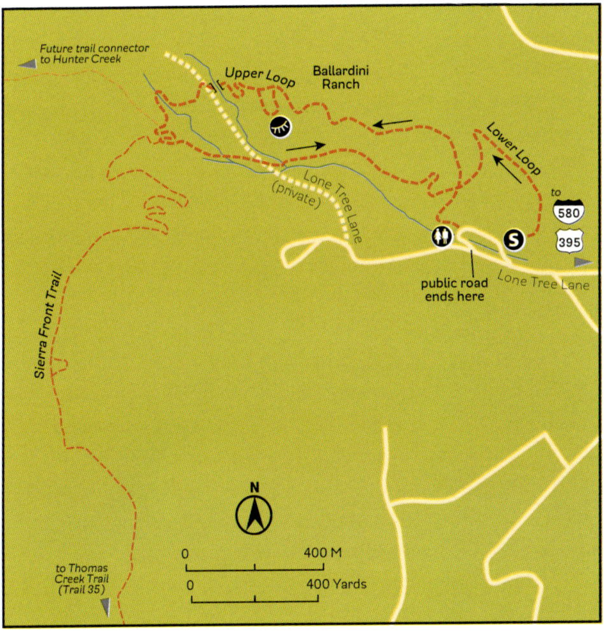

Looking west into the Sierra foothills from the Ballardini Ranch loop

GETTING THERE

Driving: From I-580 south (US Highway 395 south), take exit 30 for Neil Road (Meadowood Mall Way). Continue straight off the freeway exit onto Southbound Frontage Road. Continue for 0.4 mile, then turn right onto Neil Road. Continue for 0.1 mile, then take the second exit onto Del Monte Lane at the traffic circle. Continue for 1.4 miles, then go right on Huffaker Lane (NV 671 east). At 0.5 mile, turn left to stay on Huffaker and continue 0.5 mile. Turn right onto Lone Tree Lane and continue for 0.7 mile, then turn right into the trailhead parking lot.

This is a popular trail system, with peak hours on weekends. Ballardini is named for the Italian family who raised cattle; grew hay, grain, and vegetables here; and created an irrigation system that relies on gravity. The patriarch, Antonio, passed away in 1950 and, despite his children fighting to keep the land intact as open space, parcels were sold off. Washoe County purchased 121 acres and built this wonderful park.

Combining the park's two loops is a nice way to see everything it offers. Views from the loops vary widely, with the lower one exposing city views that stretch to Geiger Grade, and the upper taking hikers deeper into the Carson Range. June is a great time to see wildflowers and catch a quick hike before the heat sets in too much. In winter, snow and ice may be present.

Keep your eyes out for Washoe County to break ground on its proposed trail, connecting Ballardini and Thomas Creek (see Go Farther) to Hunter Creek.

GET MOVING

To start on the Lower Loop, locate the trail at the eastern end of the parking lot, marked with a break in the fence, bench, and a trail sign. This 0.4-mile section offers a lovely vista of the city and foothills, as silvery Great Basin sagebrush rolls down toward the valley, with phlox, soft lupine, and mariposa lily dispersed throughout.

Here and on the Upper Loop, the trail is quite bumpy, with loose rocks covering much of the surface in some stretches. While this can be annoying, it also gives you a chance to see the fascinating geologic history of this area up close. While you're stumbling over the rocks, see how many colors you can find within them: reds, oranges, grays, whites, and tans so light they're almost yellow, each hue signifying a unique set of mineral balances. The colors complement the dusty greens of the surrounding plants and the bright blues or moody clouds adorning the sky.

The trail switches back south at 0.3 mile, shortly arriving at the trail junction. The intersection forms an X; the left side is part of the park's Upper Loop, while the right is part of the Lower Loop. A trail sign here helps visualize that. To continue along this grand park loop, take the northwest trail to the right (or the top left arm of that X-shaped trail).

From here, the path gains double the elevation (150 feet) of the Lower Loop in 0.5 mile. Meander along this ascent to soak in the gorgeous folds and nooks of the Carson Range. At

0.9 mile, at the peak of the ascent, find a sign marking the intersection with a small 560-foot-long overlook loop featuring an eastward-facing bench. This lookout loop is the highest point of the hike. While its views are similar to those on the Lower Loop, the bench is a nice reward for completing the uphill portion of this trail. Continue along the overlook loop until it returns to the main trail, just west of where it started. Turn left and continue west. The main trail switches back twice to descend the hillside into a creek valley. At 1.1 miles, there is a small bridge to cross the water, which may or may not be flowing, depending on the time of year.

About 150 feet from the bridge, the trail is bisected by a single-lane dirt road. This is Lone Tree Lane, the same road used to access the park. Here, it is private property, as is the land just north of the trail. Walk straight across, respecting private property, and connect back with the trail. At 1.3 miles, cross another potentially flowing creek, this time with a land bridge to help. About 0.1 mile down the trail, notice the active restoration site marked by a sign asking hikers to please stay on trail. Other users have cut this switchback, but at the peril of the environment.

Continue around the trail as it switches back twice again. Here, notice a trail splitting off to the right (west). This is the Sierra Front Trail, a wonderful way to extend your hike (see Go Farther). A larger stream also appears along the south side of the trail. Here, trickling water matches the shimmer of cottonwood and aspen leaves in the ever-present breeze.

At 1.6 miles, the trail meets again with Lone Tree Lane. This time, the trail is not directly across the road; make a right and travel along Lone Tree Lane for about 90 feet before picking up the trail again to the left. At 2 miles, the trailhead parking lot becomes visible. After two switchbacks, meet again with the X intersection. This time, turn right to travel along the southwest point of this junction. A gentle 0.1-mile walk remains, dropping you into the parking lot by the restrooms.

Looking southeast from the Upper Loop as the sun sets

GO FARTHER

The Sierra Front Trail is part of a local vision to connect the entire length of the Carson Range in Reno, from Peavine to Galena. One of the newest established trails in the region, the segment between Ballardini Ranch (Trail 25) and the Lower Thomas Creek trailhead (Trail 35) was completed in summer 2022. This trail seems to be quieter, attracting fewer casual hikers.

Access this 5.6-mile (point-to-point) route at mile 1.4 on the Upper Loop, where the Sierra Front Trail begins its 1050-foot climb. Up, up, up the trail goes, around the mountain just south of Ballardini Ranch, then levels out for the most part and rewards with gorgeous, sweeping views. Walk as far as you'd like, or make the full 11.2-mile journey before returning to Ballardini Ranch.

Next page: *Wetlands are a major feature of Damonte Ranch Park (Trail 33). Pause for a while to enjoy the wide-open views and abundant wildlife.*

SPARKS AND SOUTHEAST RENO

The Southern Pacific Railroad wetlands, volcanoes, a restored aquifer, historical alfalfa ranches, wild horses, and old stagecoach roads—what could define the image of a Wild West town better than this section? Sparks and Reno are kissing cities that both developed with mining and the railroad. The Southern Pacific Railroad purchased land just southwest of the present-day Sparks Marina (Trail 27), where they built the largest roundhouse in the world at the time (and largest building west of the Mississippi) to store and service locomotives. The town was nicknamed "Rail City." Despite the development, it maintained a quieter persona as neighboring Reno ballooned into a divorce and gambling center. A 1.4-mile walk west from the Sparks Marina along Victorian Avenue commemorates this history with timely facades and cultural museums (and good food and drink!).

Farming and ranching in both cities supported growing populations, including the gold mining town of Virginia City, which was one of the most demanding. Access to and from it was serviced, in part, by the Toll Road (Trail 34). Though it has been exchanged for the Geiger Grade in our modern metropolitan area, the walk along the Toll Road can spark a sense of gold fury.

Not all hikes in this section reveal anthropocentric history. Huffaker Hills Open Space (Trail 31) is a funny little mountain that, along with nearby Huffaker Park, stands alone in the middle of the city. These represent some of the youngest volcanoes in the area, active about one million years ago. Today, their peaks provide 360-degree views and easy access from a number of neighborhoods and shops.

The Highland Loop in Hidden Valley Regional Park (Trail 28) also represents a bit of Nevada's wild landscape. Despite the manicured homes and golf course that line its entry, this park is largely undeveloped. Wild horses are a common sight, with the occasional yipping coyote cutting through social routes, reminders of how close nature truly is.

As the mountains squeeze together and the valley narrows, southeast Reno offers an incredible glimpse into the Truckee Meadows throughout its long, explosive history. With every type of adventure at the ready, this is an awesome section of town to explore.

26 Teglia's Paradise Park

DISTANCE: 1-mile loop
ELEVATION GAIN: Minimal
HIGH POINT: 4430 feet
DIFFICULTY: Easy
FITNESS: Walkers, runners, cyclists
FAMILY-FRIENDLY: Yes, ADA and stroller accessible
DOG-FRIENDLY: Yes, leashed
AMENITIES: Barbecues, picnic shelter, playground, restrooms, benches
CONTACT: City of Reno, download map from website
GPS: 39.543121°, -119.776650°
BEFORE YOU GO: Open sunrise to sunset (hours posted at entry gate)

GETTING THERE

Public Transit: Take RTC 2 to the Silverada Boulevard and Paradise Drive stop. Access the northwestern corner of the

Springtime blooms along one of the ponds at Teglia's Paradise Park

park by walking east along Paradise Drive for 590 feet where the street turns into Carville Drive.

Driving: From I-80 east, take exit 16 for Prater Way. Turn left off the freeway exit onto Prater Way and continue 0.2 mile. Turn left onto El Rancho Drive and continue for 0.4 mile, then turn left onto Elementary Drive. After 180 feet, turn right into the parking lot.

Paradise Park mirrors Virginia Lake (Trail 23) without the crowds. This former gravel pit now features four ponds separated by simple landscaping. The Nevada Department of Wildlife (NDOW) stocks the 24 surface acres of water with rainbow and brown trout, bluegill, and channel catfish. Anglers can cast from accessible fishing piers that line the north and south ponds (get a fishing license from NDOW).

Though this is one of the smallest parks in Reno (just 38 acres), pedestrians can enjoy a relaxing journey around the water. In summer, Bradford pear trees line the lakes, and the community garden is full of colors and plants. The on-site Teglia's Paradise Park Activity Center hosts recreation programs, activities, and classes. Visit the City of Reno website for a schedule of events.

GET MOVING

From the parking lot, locate the green bridge. Instead of crossing it, take a right to head north along the paved path (feel free to cross the bridge after the loop to explore the grassy areas). This main pond here has fishing docks; the others do not.

What you may notice in spring (besides the ponds) are the white flowering crabapple trees; they border most of this pond and show up sporadically around the other ponds. Summertime brings the beautiful leaves of the Russian olives, cottonwoods, and trees-of-heaven. During winter, the sights focus more on the water, where you might see mergansers, herons, coots, and grebes gliding through the ponds.

In total, there are four ponds within the park. This path traces each. At 0.1 mile, the trail curves left and heads west. Continue for another 0.1 mile until the parking lot ends and a path sprouts off to the left (south). Ignore it, and instead, head west across the parking lot, toward the playground. There are boulders here that mark the start of a short dirt path that continues around the northern shore of the third pond for 0.1 mile. Take this. It can be difficult to see the path here; hug the shore of this pond to stay on track. If accessing the park via public transportation, pick up the trail here by walking southeast from the playground to the pond.

At 0.3 mile, under a short but stately four-trunked cottonwood, the pavement picks up again and continues for about 50 feet before curving south. Walk over the footbridge,

pausing to enjoy the serene stream beneath. The trail continues south for another 0.1 mile before curving to the east around the fourth and final pond. At 0.5 mile, find Teglia's Paradise Park Activity Center, which offers various recreation programs during the week. Find a schedule of activities on the City of Reno website (see Resources).

Continue east. At 0.6 mile, the trail passes the community garden, which operates from dawn to dusk, spring through fall. (For more information, contact the City of Reno.) About 1000 feet later, the trail reaches the western end of the green bridge. Head straight to go south on the trail, around the west side of the first pond, where workout equipment is spaced out every 200 feet or so. The trail makes its way around this pond and back to the parking lot.

27 Sparks Marina Park

DISTANCE: 2-mile loop
ELEVATION GAIN: Minimal
HIGH POINT: 4400 feet
DIFFICULTY: Easy
FITNESS: Walkers, runners, cyclists
FAMILY-FRIENDLY: Yes, ADA and stroller accessible
DOG-FRIENDLY: Yes, leashed
AMENITIES: Pet waste stations, benches, off-leash dog park, showers, picnic areas, fishing pier, volleyball courts, playgrounds, concession stand (hours vary), restrooms
CONTACT: City of Sparks, download map from website
GPS: 39.534963°, -119.731617°
BEFORE YOU GO: Open 6 AM–10 PM; all-terrain wheelchairs available to access beaches and water; swimming allowed only when lifeguards are on duty

GETTING THERE

Public Transit: Take RTC 21 to the Howard Drive at Sparks Marina stop. This deposits users at the start of the trail described below.

Driving: From I-80 east, take exit 19 for McCarran Boulevard East. Turn left off the freeway onto South McCarran and continue for 0.3 mile. Turn right onto Nichols Boulevard and continue 0.2 mile. Take the third exit at the traffic circle onto Howard Drive. After 340 feet, turn right into the parking lot.

A trail between a shopping complex and freeway might not sound appealing when seeking nature, but this 2-mile loop is an easy outing. Once a gravel pit, reclamation and the 1997 flood of the Truckee River turned it into the Sparks Marina. At its center lies Helms Lake, a natural aquifer that experts estimate receives 1–3 million gallons of water daily. The City of Sparks keeps levels stable by pumping excess water into the Truckee River.

The park is busy evenings and weekends year-round, with spring and summer offering perfect sunset views. Little tree coverage makes midday in summer quite hot. Recreation opportunities endear the Sparks Marina to locals. Dogs enjoy the off-leash park, families play at sandy beaches (with sand imported from Lake Tahoe), and anglers cast for trout, bass, catfish, and carp (obtain a license from Nevada Department of Wildlife). Native plants, bird sightings, and views of both Peavine and the Carson Range await. If the trails become too crowded, take to Helms Lake with a kayak or paddleboard to enjoy views with a meditative quiet.

GET MOVING

This loop is straightforward and easy to follow, though it can be hectic at the trailhead from the Howard Drive parking lot. Notice the trail running north–south, parallel with the lot. Start here and travel south toward the parking lot's roundabout (not the roundabout where Howard Drive and Nichols Boulevard meet). At this roundabout, turn left to follow its curve for about 90 feet, where it meets with another small trail at the opening of a grassy peninsula. Turn left and continue on this northeastern path for 80 feet. Next, turn right (east) along the perimeter of the peninsula, starting a 0.2-mile lollipop loop. In this section, enjoy benches covered with pergolas, great views of the lake, and ample shade.

About 250 feet after starting around the perimeter, the trail converges, then splits again 80 feet later to create the loop part of this lollipop-loop section. About 400 feet into this peninsula loop, a trail leads left toward the boating beach. Ignore this and continue back to the trail that led you toward this loop. When the trail splits again, continue along the left. In 300 feet, it converges with the roundabout area. Turn left to continue south on the loop trail. Now the Sparks Marina path becomes self-explanatory.

At 0.5 mile, the trail curves around, heading east. This section parallels the freeway, but dense trees, including pines, separate the visual impact of traffic from the park, though noise does leak through the green coverage. Here, along the lakeside, notice the beautifully manicured grass, deciduous trees, and plenty of places to lay out a picnic. At 0.6 mile, there is a fishing pier off to the left. This spot is very popular with anglers, not leaving much room for curious walkers. Pass this by and allow the casters to enjoy their spot at the lake.

Meet with the off-leash dog park at 0.8 mile. Dogs are legally required to be leashed everywhere (unless posted) in Washoe County, and it is especially true of a popular path like this. Let your pooch run free in the dog park; it even has water access, so aquatic pups can get their swimming fill. Then leash them for the rest of the walk.

Reach the trail's easternmost point at 1 mile. Two trails converge here; the most obvious might look like the one to the left, but take the right instead. As the trail curves around

Spectacular sunset at the Sparks Marina

to the north, it borders The Outlets at Legends parking lot. At 1.1 miles, turn left to stay on the trail. It begins to border townhomes at 1.3 miles. While peeking into people's secret lives might entice you, make sure to look west at the gorgeous view of Peavine. This section is the loop's prime sunset destination, where melted oranges and pinks radiate over the mountaintop and sparkle in the water.

At 1.6 miles, make a sharp left and walk over the bridge. A small bay extends east here. About 0.1 mile later, East Lincoln Way comes into view. At 1.7 miles, the trail turns left and west, paralleling East Lincoln. This change in direction marks the start of the swimming beach. The path turns again at 1.9 miles, and a variety of intersecting and parallel paths appear. Stay on the one closest to the beach. At 2 miles, turn left back to the parking lot to end the trip.

28 Highland Loop

DISTANCE:	2.6-mile loop
ELEVATION GAIN:	Up to 330 feet
HIGH POINT:	4880 feet
DIFFICULTY:	Moderate to challenging
FITNESS:	Walkers, hikers, runners, cyclists
FAMILY-FRIENDLY:	Yes, but has steep sections with narrow tread and loose footing. See Go Farther for other options in this area.
DOG-FRIENDLY:	Yes, leashed
AMENITIES:	Pet waste stations, benches, playgrounds, off-leash dog park, picnic areas, restrooms
CONTACT:	Washoe County, download map from website
GPS:	39.490769°, –119.714505°
BEFORE YOU GO:	Open sunrise to sunset; frequent wild horse and rattlesnake sightings; some steep drop-offs

GETTING THERE

Driving: From I-80 east, take exit 20 for Sparks Boulevard and turn right. After 0.5 mile, the street turns into Veterans Parkway; continue straight. At 2 miles, turn left on Pembroke Drive. After 0.8 mile, turn right on Parkway Drive, which dead-ends at the park in 0.5 mile. Take the first left, then follow the road about 0.4 mile to the dirt parking lot.

The Highland Loop at Hidden Valley Regional Park offers a sense of freedom. Its peaks and canyons stand out from across town, its light sandy appearance, speckled with dark dots of Utah juniper trees, distinguishes it from the rest of the Virginia Range. But what truly makes Hidden Valley stand out is the sense of wilderness it provides. Only about 13 percent of the 480-acre park is developed. Wild horses roam through the sage, and the howls of coyotes ring down the soft slopes.

The Highland Loop is the highest developed trail within the park, giving users a great sense of the possibilities the area

Golden hour descends on the Highland Loop.

offers, while allowing a safe and easy(ish) to navigate route. The park's three other developed trails require less energy commitments (see Go Farther).

GET MOVING

From the parking lot, take the small dirt path leading east, in line with the gate in the fence on the eastern side of the park. The fence is to prevent the horses from entering the neighborhood, but they travel where they want here. Gates at points along the fencing provide access for hikers and cyclists, and each operates a little differently. The gate here overlaps slightly, creating a gap you shimmy through.

Once inside, travel about 400 feet east, then turn right on a southbound trail, at the Highland Loop sign. Such markers

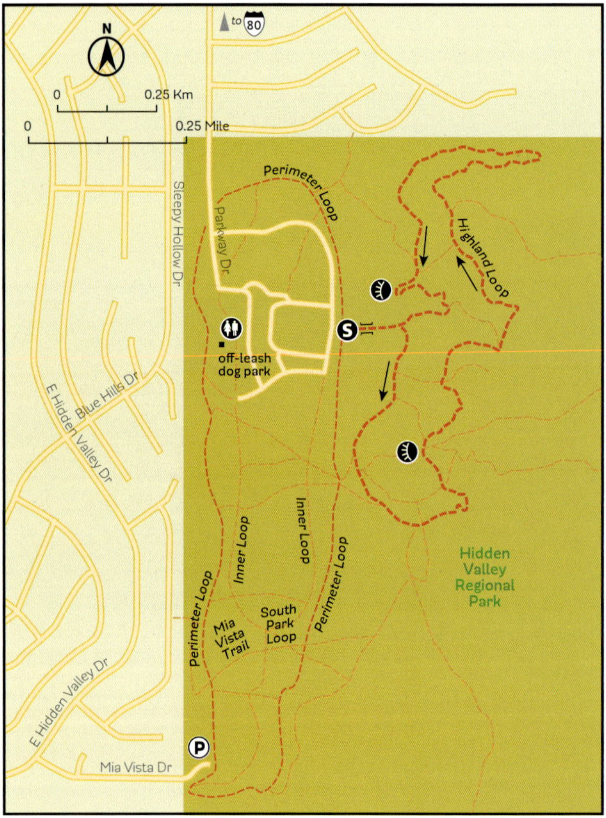

appear periodically to keep you on track. Begin a slow ascent to the trail's peak, about 240 feet up in 0.9 mile. You get a brief break from traveling uphill 0.2 mile in, where an east–west trail intersects. Continue straight (south). In 50 feet, two more trails sprout off. This is a common occurrence at Hidden Valley and can make even the simplest trail an adventure. Here, keep along the leftmost (east) trail.

In 100 more feet, come to a social trail spur that can be confusing. Stay on the trail on the right (southwest), the one that keeps at a steady elevation. At 0.3 mile, follow the rightmost trail (southwest) again. In another 300 feet, reach a sign pointing to the left (eastern) trail and follow it. Signs like these "point" to the correct way by placing the panel in the direction of the trail. For example, if the trail goes west, hikers looking at the post's information would also face west. This is an incredibly helpful tool for trails like this.

Continue another 0.1 mile to where the trail reaches a sandy valley. This is the most frazzling section. Locate the official trail on the southernmost side of the valley, the one hugging the opposite hill. Follow it southeast toward the orange-colored mountains for 0.1 mile. Cross a shallow drainage and turn slightly left to rejoin an eastbound trail. You should spot a trail marker from here. Let this guide you through the remaining 500 feet of valley floor.

Congratulations on making it up out of the valley. As a reward, the trail ascends (about 50 feet in 0.1 mile), but it is easier to follow from here forward. Watch your step; the trail has dramatic outslopes in sections that fall down short yet steep canyons. At 0.8 mile, another east–west trail intersects; stay straight (north). In about 260 feet, the first of three trails pop off to the left (west). These take users to the top of the hill for an overlook. Many enjoy this vista, but it seems superfluous, since the trail offers comparable views. At 0.9 mile, about 20 feet after the last of the overlook trails, the loop curves east, circumnavigating the hill. Ignore the trail heading north, and continue east. Here, the environment changes slightly. Notice how the rocks have that same deep red as the ones high above the Hunter Creek Falls Trail (Trail 20)? This is due to iron-rich minerals.

Another trail crosses at 1 mile, which extends up a sharp pitch to the east—an obvious deterrent, unless you crave an ass-kicking blast of climbing. Continue straight (northeast) about 50 feet before coming to a rocky section. Be mindful of your step. After clearing the rocks, the trail travels east into a canyon. Here, Utah juniper and singleleaf pinyon pines line the trail, offering a brief moment of shade. Slow down and look for native wildflowers, like longleaf phlox and Humboldt Mountains milkweed in May.

The trail skirts the hillside before opening up again at 1.3 miles. A few more trail crossings might temp you to take a westward or eastward path, but remain straight on the route that heads north. At 1.5 miles, the trail curves to the east, revealing views of the neighborhood below. Here the trail is wide open, sandy, and finally away from the cliff's edge. In 0.2 mile, the trail switches back to the west. Here it is lined with a rock path and marked with a sign. The trail meanders around the hillside until returning southbound, gaining a bit of elevation.

At 2.2 miles, the official trail map directs you to take the easternmost trail. I advise against this, as it is steep and rocky. Instead, take the trail to the right (west) that switches back to the east. About 220 feet after the switchback, continue straight east instead of down the hillside. This takes you to the Highlands Loop at 2.3 miles, where the trail winds down the hillside and joins a westward trail in the valley. Take this trail right (west); you'll see the gate you entered the park through from here. Head toward it—you've just completed the Highland Loop!

GO FARTHER

The park features four main trails, including the short 0.8-mile South Park Loop. The Perimeter Loop is a great way to add more mileage. About 2.5 miles long and relatively flat, it circles the lower portion of the park. To start, find the trail that runs north–south, near the beginning of the Highland Loop, about 100 feet west of the gate, and follow it either direction.

NEVADA'S WILD HORSES

Ten thousand years ago, horses were native to this land (along with ancient relatives to cheetahs and camels). However, the ones roaming Nevada now are the descendants of domesticated horses brought here and released by European explorers, ranchers, and miners. In 2024, there were an estimated 33,400 horses roaming Bureau of Land Management (BLM) land in the state. Nevada has the highest number of roaming horses by far; Wyoming holds second place with 10,300. Over 3000 horses live within the Virginia Range alone. They do well here—almost too well—as overpopulation is an issue with some of the state's herds.

Since the Virginia Range is not managed by BLM, the horses are technically referred to as "feral" and not wild, though the BLM herds are called "wild." This nomenclature does nothing but cause confusion.

Horses can be seen at McCarran Ranch Preserve (Trail 3), along Erica Greif Bikeway (Trail 30), and Washoe Lake State Park (see Trails 39 and 40). However, there is perhaps no better place to get a sighting than Hidden Valley. Fourteen distinct coat types have been identified across the state, ranging from red to tan with black spots. How many can you find along the trail at Hidden Valley Regional Park?

In a 2018 poll by the Public Policy Polling firm, 86 percent of Nevadans reported that wild horses represent the rugged, independent culture of the state. But no matter how majestic or magical these animals seem, they are not to be approached or fed. They have unpredictable demeanors that will pave the way to a heinous emergency room visit.

29 Rosewood Nature Study Area

DISTANCE: Up to 2.5 miles, loop
ELEVATION GAIN: Minimal
HIGH POINT: 4390 feet
DIFFICULTY: Easy
FITNESS: Walkers
FAMILY-FRIENDLY: Yes
DOG-FRIENDLY: No
AMENITIES: Pet waste stations, benches, restrooms and water at visitor center
CONTACT: Truckee Meadows Parks Foundation, download map from website
GPS: 39.497756°, -119.731344°
BEFORE YOU GO: Open 8 AM–4 PM Mon., and 8 AM–7 PM Tues.–Sat. Fishing is prohibited on west side of Veterans Parkway.

GETTING THERE

Public Transit: Take RTC 54 to the South McCarran Boulevard at Emigrant Storage stop. Walk south on McCarran for 0.1 mile, then turn left onto Pembroke Drive. Continue for 0.9 mile and turn right into the trailhead parking lot.

Driving: From I-80 east, take exit 20 for Sparks Boulevard. Turn right off the freeway exit and continue on Sparks. In 0.5 mile, continue straight as Sparks turns into Veterans Parkway. Continue another 2 miles, then turn right onto Pembroke Drive. After about 0.1 mile, make the first left into the parking lot.

One of the newest additions to Reno's greater trail system is the Rosewood Nature Study Area. Truckee Meadows Parks Foundation (TMPF) restored this wetland from an old golf course and opened it to the public in 2021 with 2.9 miles of trails. TMPF's goal was to rehabilitate the lost wetland, making it a home for migrating birds, aquatic animals, and plants.

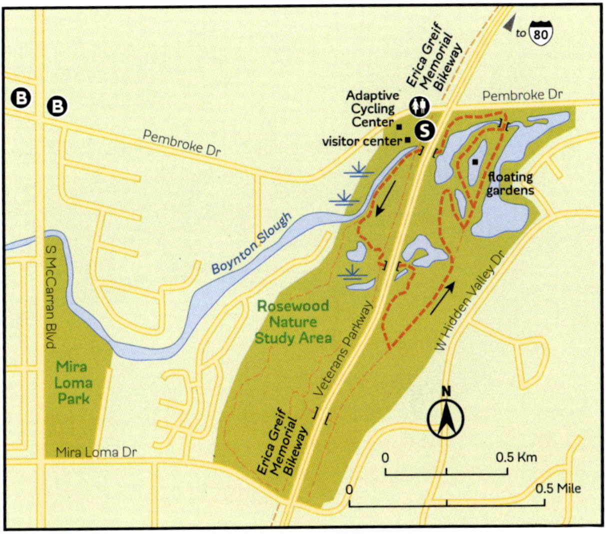

While any time of year is lovely here, migratory birds and bald eagles visit in winter.

Start at the on-site visitor center (9 AM–6 PM, Tues.–Sat.) to find taxidermy birds, a kids corner, books, mammal pelts to touch, photos, and maps of property. The best reason to visit is to meet Peavine Pete, the resident desert tortoise. An off-road wheelchair is available for free to explore the area. You can also borrow binoculars.

For a 2.5-mile journey, follow the main trail and the loop additions and explore the pollinator gardens. If you need something shorter, follow just the main trail, which is 1.7 miles.

GET MOVING

The trail starts from the back of the visitor center, though you can also walk around the west side of the center to access the trail. Notice that there are some paths leading west into a pollinator garden; feel free to explore this at your leisure. To access the trails through the wetland, locate the bridge

The trail starts from the visitor center with a bridge over Boynton Slough and gorgeous views of Mount Rose.

across Boynton Slough (also sometimes referred to as Dry Creek). This waterway is wide and deep—40 feet at its maximum depth and nearly 60 feet at its maximum width. In fact, east of Veterans Parkway, it is a fantastic place to catch carp and largemouth bass.

Cross the bridge and follow the trail as it parallels Boynton Slough. Numbered signs correspond to a self-guided tour map, which you can download from the Truckee Meadows Parks Foundation website. At 0.2 mile, notice a bridge heading west. Continue straight along the trail. In 320 feet, it splits, but the trail to the right is closed to the public because the area is still being restored by TMPF; the habitat is fragile here.

Continue along the open trail to the left as it gracefully meanders southeast. At 0.4 mile, you will see marker 5, which indicates native plants. Since 2019, the foundation and partners have planted more than 1500 native species here, including silver buffaloberry, showy penstemon, and blue flax. Continue along the trail. In about 450 feet, it ducks under Veterans Parkway to access the east side.

The trail begins to head south and then curves back north. At 1 mile, find marker 9, which points out bird boxes. Because there are few trees here (although TMPF has planted some), bird boxes encourage nesting for birds like swallows, wrens, American kestrels, and barn owls. Keep your eyes to the sky: can you spot any of these birds?

Immediately following this marker, the trail splits to create a small loop to the left. Take this 0.3-mile loop—or continue straight for 0.1 mile, where the loop connects back. About 480 feet down the trail, another 0.3-mile loop breaks off to the left of the main trail. Use the loop to see the floating gardens (marker 12), where square containers float on the wetland surface to allow growth of aquatic plants like broadleaf cattail, Baltic rush, and Nebraska sedge in an area that would otherwise be too deep.

Decide to take this loop or continue straight for 0.2 mile on the main trail. At 1.4 miles, cross a bridge over the Boynton Slough again. Before crossing, however, be sure to note marker 13, which explains the pollinator houses installed by the Help Save the Bees Foundation to house bees that nest. Across the bridge, the trail again passes under Veterans Parkway (at 1.6 miles) before returning to the trailhead, about 0.1 mile later.

GO FARTHER

Connect to the Erica Greif Memorial Bikeway (Trail 30) to continue this wetland exploration to Steamboat Creek, just southeast of Rosewood Nature Study Area. The creek flows from Washoe Lake to the Truckee River, eventually contributing to Pyramid Lake.

To access the bikeway, walk from the visitor center to Pembroke Drive. Along the western side of the intersection with Veterans Parkway, look for the protected bike path. Take it north to visit the Truckee River and Tahoe-Pyramid Trail (about 2.2 miles one-way) or south to walk along Steamboat Springs (about 3.6 miles one-way to South Meadows Parkway).

30 Erica Greif Memorial Bikeway

DISTANCE:	11.9 miles roundtrip
ELEVATION GAIN:	320 feet
HIGH POINT:	4440 feet
DIFFICULTY:	Easy to moderate
FITNESS:	Walkers, runners, cyclists
FAMILY-FRIENDLY:	Yes, ADA and stroller accessible
DOG-FRIENDLY:	Yes, leashed
AMENITIES:	Benches, trash cans, restrooms, and water at Rosewood Nature Study Area Visitor Center (during park hours only)
CONTACT:	City of Sparks, City of Reno, and Washoe County; download RTC's interactive bike map
GPS:	39.497756°, -119.731344°
BEFORE YOU GO:	Requires walking or biking to access bikeway. The Adaptive Cycling Center is near the Rosewood Nature Study Area (Trail 29) and provides rentals for people needing adaptive equipment.

GETTING THERE

Public Transit: Take RTC 54 to the South McCarran Boulevard at Emigrant Storage stop. Walk south on McCarran for 0.1 mile, then turn left onto Pembroke Drive. Continue for 1 mile where the road intersects Veterans Parkway. Turn right onto the paved path to start your adventure.

Driving: From I-80 east, take exit 20 for Sparks Boulevard. Turn right off the freeway and continue on Sparks. In 0.5 mile, continue straight as Sparks turns into Veterans Parkway. Continue for another 2 miles, then turn right onto Pembroke Drive. After about 0.1 mile, make the first left into the parking lot. Alternate parking is available at Cottonwood Park along the Truckee River at 777 Spice Island Drive, Sparks; or at Cyan Park at 2121 Long Meadow Drive, Reno.

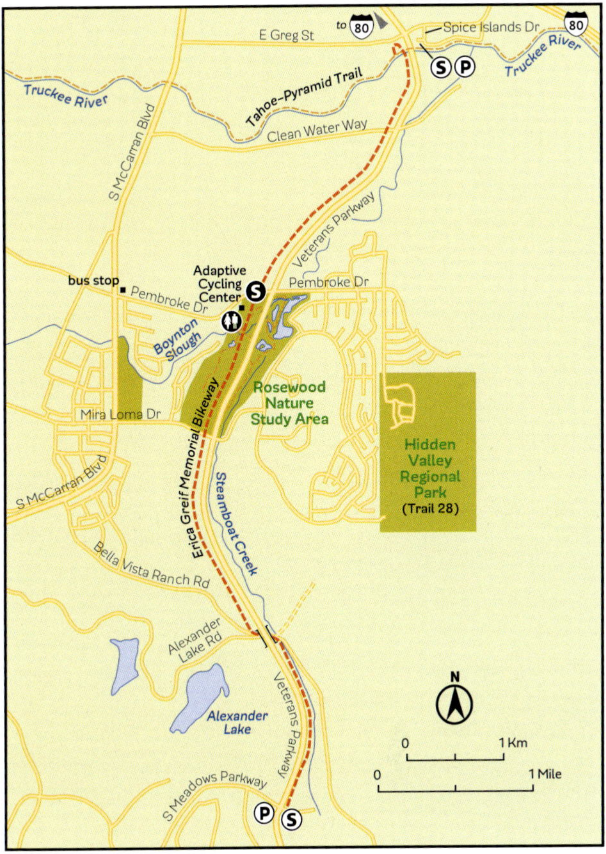

The Southeast Connector Bikeway runs from the Truckee River, at the convergence of Sparks Boulevard and Veterans Parkway, to South Meadows Parkway and is dedicated to Erica Greif. Nicknamed "The Reno Rocket," Greif was a fixture in the local cycling community and an aspiring professional cycler. She died in a car crash in 2015 on the way to the Redlands Bicycle Classic race in Highland, California.

Though the bikeway travels along the busy Veterans Parkway, it is a lovely walk, run, or ride. Along the southern portion, it diverges from Veterans Parkway to travel along open grazing land, a wetland, and the robust Steamboat Creek. Here, backing up to the foothills of the Virginia Range, wild horses are a common sight. Along the northern portion, look for wildlife like marmots and jackrabbits. From any direction, enjoy views of Mount Rose, Peavine, and Hidden Valley peaks.

GET MOVING

From the Rosewood Nature Study Area parking lot, follow Pembroke Drive east to the intersection of Veterans Parkway. Locate the bikeway on the west side of Veterans and take it. Along here, the trail borders the Rosewood wetlands. From this elevated vantage point, the foliage, water, and wildlife make a spectacular sight, especially with Mount Rose glowing in the background.

At 1 mile, reach Mira Loma Drive. Here, pedestrians and cyclists both use the sidewalk to cross. The road has right turn lanes either turning onto the Mira Loma or onto Veterans Parkway. Use extreme caution, as motorists might not see you. Cross Mira Loma and continue.

Over the next 1.4 miles, travel along a pasture and look for grazing cattle. In early spring, calves run through their mother's legs, playful and carefree—a unique sight within city limits. Benches at 1.7 miles grant space to sit and take in the view. There are periodic benches along the trail, each with a different view and stunning scenery. The trail undulates in elevation, gaining no more than about 30 feet on a given "hill." Throughout the entire trail, which gains *and* loses about 320 feet, there are short sprints like this between 2 and 2.4 miles.

Go through an underpass and come to Alexander Lake Road at 2.5 miles. Traffic has the right of way here; stop and look both directions for large work trucks and heavy machinery driving along this road. Cross and enjoy the first sights of

Views of Mount Rose and Slide Mountain are beautiful from the bikeway.

Steamboat Creek, a (confusingly) different waterway than the popular Steamboat Ditch (Trail 22). The hills to the east are home to many wild horses; though this is private property, it connects to Hidden Valley and offers an easy place for horses to migrate for water access. You may see a few grazing or visiting the creek. Remember, these are *wild* animals with unpredictable actions—do not approach them under any circumstances.

Benches at 3.1 miles face west with a perfect view of Mount Rose and Slide Mountain. Continue south along the path for another 0.6 mile until it dead-ends at South Meadows Parkway. A sidewalk and bike lane continue south from here, along Veterans Parkway, which can be used to access Cyan Park. For this trip, though, turn around and head back north for 3.7 miles to Pembroke Drive. Be cautious crossing Pembroke; there is another separated right turn lane onto Veterans. Don't expect cars to stop for you. After crossing, continue north.

At 8.2 miles, find another set of benches, facing east with gorgeous views of the sandy, pinyon-speckled Hidden Valley peaks. Just 0.6 mile north of these benches, come to the Clean Water Way crossing. Be cautious when crossing this small two-lane road.

Continue north, watching the fields to the west, which are overrun by marmots, a giant ground squirrel. They have light fur along their chest and stomach, tiny ears, and short legs.

You might notice them still as statues, catching the sunshine. They blend in well with the honey-colored grasses, so it takes a keen eye to spot one. Raptors, like eagles and hawks, can also be seen here, especially during winter.

At 9.4 miles, gain the last stretch of elevation (only about 25 feet) over the Truckee River. The path switches back down toward the river and, at 9.7 miles, meets the Idlewild to Wingfield Park Trail (Trail 2). From here, return south to Pembroke and the Rosewood Nature Study Area.

GO FARTHER

Visit the other Hidden Valley–area trails (Trail 28 and 29) easily from the Erica Greif Memorial Bikeway. To access Hidden Valley Regional Park, drive east along Pembroke for 0.9 mile, then turn right onto Parkway Drive and follow it 0.5 mile into the park. To visit Rosewood Nature Study Area, return to the parking lot you started in at Pembroke Drive, where the Rosewood Visitor Center stands. The trails begin on the other side of the visitor center.

ADAPTIVE CYCLING CENTER

The Adaptive Cycling Center, part of the City of Reno's adaptive sports program, can be found in the Rosewood Nature Study Area parking lot on Pembroke Drive. People who need adaptive bikes can rent them here for $30 (or $100 for unlimited rides). Financial assistance is available if this price is a barrier. There is equipment to suit both children and adults.

Cyclists can use them to access any bike-friendly trail in the area, including the Erica Greif Memorial Bikeway. Ride the nearby Tahoe-Pyramid Trail (Trails 1–3) or the one at Hidden Valley Regional Park (Trail 28). The center is open seasonally May–September on Tuesdays from 8 AM–5 PM, Thursdays from 8 AM–12 PM, and Saturdays from 8 AM–5 PM. Reservations outside of these hours can be made by calling (775) 333-7765.

31 Huffaker Hills Loop

DISTANCE:	3-mile loop
ELEVATION GAIN:	420 feet
HIGH POINT:	4840 feet
DIFFICULTY:	Moderate
FITNESS:	Walkers, hikers, runners, cyclists
FAMILY-FRIENDLY:	Yes
DOG-FRIENDLY:	Yes, leashed
AMENITIES:	Pet waste stations, benches, picnic area, restrooms
CONTACT:	Washoe County, download map from website
GPS:	39.466744°, -119.753560°
BEFORE YOU GO:	Open sunrise to sunset (hours posted at entry gate); rattlesnakes sighted here; no water available

GETTING THERE

Driving: From I-580 south (US Highway 395 south), take exit 31 for South Virginia Street (Kietzke Lane). Stay right to take the South Virginia Street ramp. Turn left off the freeway exit, and make another immediate left onto South McCarran Boulevard. In 1.4 miles, make the first right onto Alexander Lake Road. (This junction can be hard to spot.) Continue for 1.1 miles, then turn right into the trailhead parking lot. Note: the road is private just after the trailhead access.

This area has deep historical significance for the Washoe people—artifacts date human activity here for 1500 years. The Thomas, Whites, and Steamboat Creeks flowed into the valley east of the Huffaker Hills, creating a giant green marsh. The once-diverse ecosystem, providing food and materials for construction and basketry, is now a space associated with the high desert.

Today, it remains partially open to the public. The Huffaker volcanoes are split into two separate open spaces: Huffaker Hills and Huffaker Park. This loop focuses on Huffaker Hills. Though regionally close, the trailheads are not within walking distance of each other. This loop lies within Huffaker Hills, the larger mountain situated northeast, providing incredible 360-degree views of the city and surrounding mountains. The area is exposed; be cautious of heat and sun. The best times to visit are dry days from October to May, when temperatures are palatable. Be sure to hike in April, when purple Beckwith's violets carpet the landscape.

Washoe County has plans to build another trail here to connect the two high points of the mountain; keep your ears open for updates.

GET MOVING

From the parking lot, locate the trails behind the kiosk. Take the Lakeview Loop on the far left (southeast). About 150 feet in, the Huffaker Reservoir comes into view. This is a private reservoir for irrigation, though it sits in a naturally formed basin. Although the water is locked behind a barbed wire fence, it is still a lovely sight, like an oasis in the desert.

At 0.3 mile, the trail splits at a signed junction. Continue straight (southeast) for 0.1 mile to get a full view of the reservoir, then return to the trail junction. Take the trail that forks to the left (southwest) and begins to gain elevation (about 50 feet in 0.2 mile). At the end of this little uphill push, around 0.6 mile, arrive at another signed junction. Here, turn left to head south toward the peak. Keep an eye out for bighead clover, Beckwith's violet, Hooker's balsamroot, and twinleaf onion, which usually bloom in late April and early May.

The trail begins its approach to the lookout at 0.8 mile, gaining about 160 feet of elevation in 0.4 mile. Here, notice planes taking off from the nearby Reno-Tahoe International Airport. If you have little ones who are fascinated by planes, this is a fun place to watch them—the peak even has a lovely bench facing the airport.

Rest at the peak and enjoy views of Peavine and Rattlesnake Mountains

Around 0.9 mile, the hill itself provides some shade in the afternoon, a welcome relief on sunny days. This area can be very warm, even as early as April. At 1.1 miles, a social trail on the left (southwest) cuts the switchback. Please disregard this and stay on the trail, both to help the fragile environment continue to thrive and to keep you from any rattlesnake hiding in overgrown sagebrush or under rocks.

In another 0.1 mile, a second social trail veers off to the right (west). From this point, there are a handful of them that can be confusing. Stay on the trail that most closely hugs the mountain peak.

Here, at 1.2 miles, enjoy the incredible views from the peak before backtracking 0.6 mile to the Lakeview Loop. At the intersection, turn left (northwest), then travel 0.1 mile to meet with the Western Loop at 2 miles. Turn left to head southwest here. The next 0.4 mile snakes down the hill, losing about 90 feet of elevation. The trail is rocky, so watch your step. At 2.4 miles, come to an intersection and keep to the right (north). There is private land south and west of here, so although

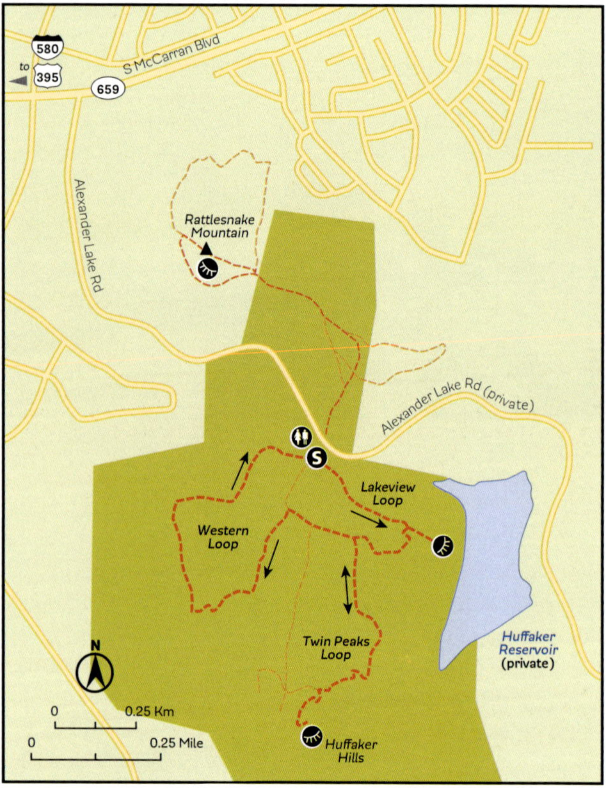

you may see trails, please be respectful and stay within the Washoe County designated areas. At 2.6 miles, reach another junction. Again, take a right here, beginning a leisurely journey east back toward the trailhead.

GO FARTHER

Rattlesnake Mountain, just across Alexander Lake Road, is a challenging but fantastic way to extend this adventure. Don't be afraid of the name; there are no more rattlesnakes here than anywhere else in this book.

From the Huffaker Hills trailhead, cross the road to the north and locate the green gate. Follow the large jeep road east and north. After passing through a gate at the base of the summit, the real uphill battle starts. In total, gain 400 feet of elevation along the 0.7-mile trek to the top, where an incredible 360-degree panorama knocks the view from Huffaker out of the water.

32 South Meadows Neighborhood Paths

DISTANCE:	3.9-mile loop
ELEVATION GAIN:	50 feet
HIGH POINT:	4490 feet
DIFFICULTY:	Easy
FITNESS:	Walkers, runners
FAMILY-FRIENDLY:	Yes, ADA and stroller accessible
DOG-FRIENDLY:	Yes, leashed
AMENITIES:	Pet waste stations, benches, Little Free Library
CONTACT:	City of Reno, download map from website
GPS:	39.4308395°, -119.7472329°
BEFORE YOU GO:	These are neighborhood paths; respect private property and keep children and dogs close.

GETTING THERE

Public Transit: Take RTC 56 to the Double R Boulevard and Double Diamond Parkway stop. Walk for 0.3 mile, then turn right onto Wilbur May Parkway. Walk for another 0.3 mile to Center Creek Park.

Driving: From I-580 south (US Highway 395 south), take exit 26 for Damonte Ranch Parkway. Turn left off the freeway exit, then continue for 0.3 mile. Use the second from the left lane to turn left onto Double R Boulevard, then take the first right on Double Diamond Parkway. Continue for 0.3 mile, then turn right onto Wilbur May Parkway. In 0.3 mile, turn left into the Center Creek Park parking lot.

South Meadows has thriving wetlands and is home to hundreds of different species of birds, plants, amphibians, and more. This healthy habitat makes an excellent place to look for birds like the white-faced ibis, yellow-headed blackbird, American avocet, red-winged blackbird, American coot, eared grebe, and black-crowned night heron.

The paved paths are ADA compliant, easy for families, and perfect for strolls of any length. Though this is a neighborhood trail, its proximity to major businesses, office complexes, and shops makes it a great jaunt to enjoy on lunch breaks, while running errands, or after doctor appointments.

GET MOVING

From Center Creek Park, locate the trail on the eastern side of the creek, about 400 feet from the parking lot. Though other park paths may eventually lead here, this is the most direct way to begin the adventure.

This segment frequently splits into small trails to the neighborhoods. These paths are not mentioned, as it should be obvious which is the main trail and which dead-end. If you do take a wrong turn, these neighborhood connectors are short, and it is easy to get back to the main route.

As the trail maintains its northern journey, it flirts with the creek, crossing multiple times and giving users the opportunity to experience the beautiful wetlands up close. They are fragile habitats. Please keep dogs and children (and fiery adults) out of the water and on the trail, to protect the environment. At 0.6 mile, come to Comstock Park, the second of three parks on this loop. This is the last place to find a restroom, though it may be closed in winter. Continue straight for 0.1 mile, then cross Carat Avenue. There is a crosswalk, but do be careful. Continue straight (north) from here.

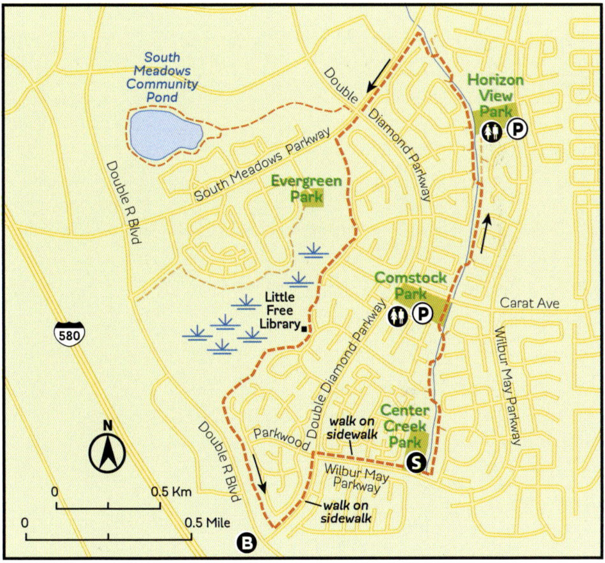

At 1.2 miles, the trail makes a Y. The right side of this Y connects to Horizon View Park, the final park on this journey. If you are not interested in visiting it, continue on the left side of the Y as it crosses the creek. The trail dead-ends at South Meadows Parkway at 1.6 miles. Here, the tranquil path gives way to a sidewalk along the busy road. (This is short-lived; after 0.4 mile, it enters back into green space.) Turn left to head southwest along the road, crossing Double Diamond Parkway after 0.3 mile.

Shortly after, keep an eye out to the south for a mural along the wall, separating the neighborhood from the road. Here, turn left (south), away from South Meadows Parkway. The next 1.4 miles opens up into a large wetland with amazing views of Mount Rose. The path curves around the border of a neighborhood in this section, and at 3.2 miles, find a Little Free Library. If a book catches your eye, there is a lovely grassy space in 0.1 mile, and again in 0.3 mile, to sit and read.

This walk along wetlands in South Meadows makes the city feel miles away.

At 3.4 miles, the trail meets Double Diamond Parkway again. Turn left and follow it northeast for 0.3 mile. Cross Parkwood Drive, then turn right to cross Double Diamond Parkway. Continue for another 0.3 mile until you return to Center Creek Park.

GO FARTHER

From the first Double Diamond Parkway crossing at 2.3 miles, continue 200 feet northwest along Double Diamond instead of continuing along South Meadows Parkway. Here, make a left on a paved path. In 0.4 mile, reach South Meadows Community Pond. A pleasant 0.8-mile walk around the pond is relaxing and a great way to see more waterfowl and riparian plants. Retrace your steps back to Double Diamond Parkway, then resume the loop above by turning right on South Meadows Parkway and following the rest of the trail description.

33 Damonte Ranch Park

DISTANCE:	3.3-mile loop
ELEVATION GAIN:	Minimal
HIGH POINT:	4490 feet
DIFFICULTY:	Easy
FITNESS:	Walkers, runners, cyclists
FAMILY-FRIENDLY:	Yes, ADA and stroller accessible
DOG-FRIENDLY:	Yes, leashed
AMENITIES:	Pet waste stations, playground, basketball court, walking paths, picnic shelter, barbecue area, tables and benches, restrooms
CONTACT:	Damonte Ranch HOA
GPS:	39.42526°, -119.72746°
BEFORE YOU GO:	Trail is public but managed by Damonte Ranch Homeowners Association (HOA). Respect posted signs and private property. Stay on trail; do not enter wetland areas.

GETTING THERE

Driving: From I-580 south (US Highway 395 south), take exit 26 for Damonte Ranch Parkway. Turn left off the freeway and follow Damonte Ranch Parkway for 0.7 mile. Turn left on Steamboat Parkway and continue for 0.8 mile. Turn right into Damonte Ranch Park.

This roughly 3-mile loop is a great introduction to the wetland areas in south Reno, with beautiful views of the surrounding mountains—including Mount Rose, Peavine, and the Virginia Range—along an easy paved pathway. Like many of the wetland areas in town, it also offers amazing opportunities for bird-watching, especially in spring. Expect to see or hear the calls of marsh wrens, sparrows, a variety of ducks, willets, California gulls, American avocets, and white-faced ibis. To learn more, attend a Lahontan Audubon Society event here (see Resources).

Between the mountain backdrop and foreground buzz of birds, it is easy to forget this area lies immediately off a major throughway. The trail listed below is just the start—there are about 9 more miles of pathways in the area to help you soak up that dose of nature.

GET MOVING

From Damonte Ranch Park, locate the trail just beyond the restrooms and basketball court, at the southwest end of the park. Turn right to follow the path counterclockwise as it winds around the neighborhood. When the wetland opens up, it offers a beautiful distraction from all the homes. At 0.3 mile, reach the first of many scenic stone benches for admiring the view. This particular one looks out over a pond to Mount Rose towering in the distance.

The trail meanders west until 0.6 mile, at the Veterans Parkway overpass. The trail forks, with one small trail on the left venturing under the road and across to more wetlands west. It can sometimes be flooded in spring and should not be attempted during these times. The northern fork on the right accesses Veterans Parkway. Take this second trail and approach the road, then turn left and head south for 0.2 mile on the sidewalk along the parkway.

The trail resumes again on the other side of the overpass. Turn left to head eastward from Veterans Parkway into the wetland again. In just under 800 feet, reach a neighborhood path, the first of four along this southern half of the loop. This leg looks east to the Virginia Range.

Notice the dotted hills: this is the pinyon-juniper forest gradually filling in the environment. Singleleaf pinyon pine nuts were an important food source for Indigenous peoples in the area. Pine nuts that we buy in the store today mostly come from Colorado pinyon, but singleleaf pine nuts are still harvested. Traditionally, the nuts are ground and made into a soup, mush, or cake. You may also notice the large white D on

Looking east over a lush pond toward the Virginia Range

the hillside. This, like other letter signs across the city, marks the adjacent school. In this case, it represents Damonte Ranch High School.

At 1.7 miles, a delightful offshoot heads directly west. It feels like the natural direction of the trail because it continues straight, versus the actual trail that begins to curve northeast. This 0.2-mile trip takes users farther into the wetland, where a semicircle of benches offers amazing views of the Sierra, from Peavine in the north to Mount Rose in the south.

The trail continues to circumnavigate the neighborhood. At 2 miles, reach the last of the four neighborhood connection trails along the southern side of the loop. Just after passing this landmark, a lush pond comes into view, with a

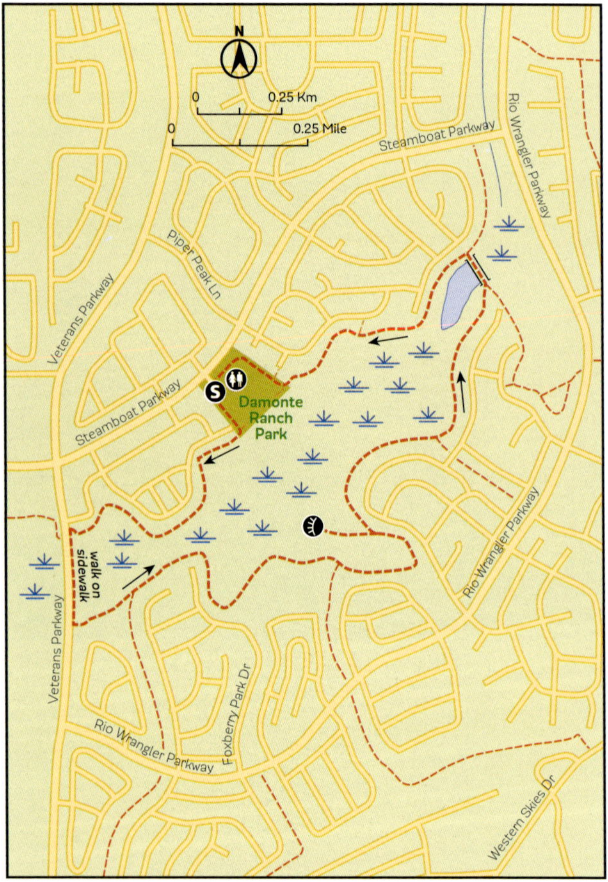

bridge spanning its width. It is an idyllic scene, especially for a neighborhood trail.

At 2.3 miles, the trail arrives at an intersection. Left is the bridge, right is another trail leading back through the neighborhood. Head left (north) to cross the bridge, enjoying the moments along it to look down into the wetland at the birds and plants that call this place home. Search for the American avocet, great egret, cinnamon teal, willet, and similar water-loving birds. After crossing the bridge, the trail splits again. Head to the left (west) for a final 0.7 mile to complete the loop.

GO FARTHER

Continue your walk through the neighborhood. In total, there are nearly 9 miles of additional trails (see the map for connecting neighborhood trails), snaking primarily southwest. Some wander farther into the wetlands, while others act as throughways for neighborhood access.

34 Toll Road Trail

DISTANCE:	5.6 miles roundtrip
ELEVATION GAIN:	1310 feet
HIGH POINT:	6380 feet
DIFFICULTY:	Challenging
FITNESS:	Walkers, hikers, runners, cyclists
FAMILY-FRIENDLY:	No, steep downhill sections with slippery tread and loose rock and shared trail with OHV users
DOG-FRIENDLY:	Yes, leashed
AMENITIES:	None
CONTACT:	Nevada Off-Highway Vehicles Program, download map from website
GPS:	39.3709138°, -119.7004726°
BEFORE YOU GO:	No amenities; pack out trash. Popular with OHVs, cars, and dirt bikes; step off trail to let OHV users pass.

GETTING THERE

Driving: From I-580 south (US Highway 395 south), take exit 25B for Virginia Street South. Continue onto US 395 ALT south for 0.5 mile. Turn left onto NV 341 east (Geiger Grade Road) toward Virginia City, making the first exit from the traffic circle. After 0.7 mile, turn right onto Toll Road. Drive 2.9 miles. When the road reaches a Y, take the right side, where there is space for four to five cars. Another parking area is farther east, but should only be accessed with high-clearance, four-wheel drive vehicles.

When researching trails for this book, I initially passed on the Toll Road: It's an old wagon route that motorized users still enjoy. It has a straightforward (boring) route that leads to—but doesn't arrive at—Virginia City. Why would someone be interested in this trail? Dear hiker, I hope you don't make the same mistake. This road is full of surprises, like the healthy Jeffrey pine forest or the intense blaze of the sunset; it's a perfect example of the hidden wonders of the Great Basin that so often gets painted as nothing more than brown hills and wastelands. But there's an adventure to unlock here that should not be disregarded.

This trail is rated as challenging because of the sketchy footing when descending. The ascent is moderate and manageable; it's the downhill that gets tricky. Loose rocks and sloped sections can make footing difficult. Bring trekking poles if you are not confident.

GET MOVING

From the main parking area, the trail should be immediately obvious because it is a continuation of the primitive road heading east. The "trail" will be this width and consistency all the way up, with growing ruts after particularly wet winters.

As you begin your trek eastward, the most notable feature is the rocky peak of Owl Rock to the south. This hilltop, a regional hub for outdoor sport climbing, has been used recreationally since the 1970s, so it is very possible you will see someone climbing or rappelling. At 0.2 mile, a trail splits off to the right (south), leading to Owl Rock. Continue on Toll Road.

The next feature that stands out are the pine trees, a surprising towering forest tucked into this canyon. Ponderosa

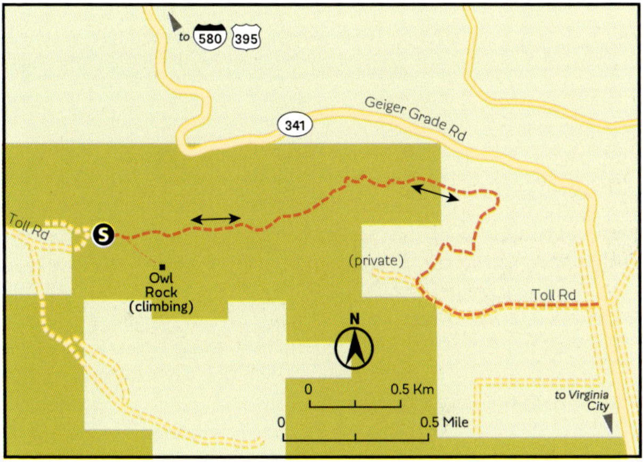

and Jeffrey pines mix with pinyon pines, both singleleaf and juniper. Across the lower Virginia Range, this feels like a rarity and adds to the specialness of this area. It also provides some shade. While looking up at the sky-reaching canopy, keep an eye out for birds of prey like hawks and golden eagles. Don't forget to look down, too, not only to watch your step around the loose rock and uneven tread, but also to search for blooms like the white three-petaled mariposa lily, deep purple penstemon, or yellow sunflower.

The trail follows a steady grade up the mountain. Expect to gain about 200–300 feet each half mile. Funnily enough, this peaceful trail was known as "Robber Roost" because the grade and its sharp turns (like the ones around the 1-mile mark) caused drivers to slow down enough to be overtaken by stagecoach robbers. At 0.6 mile, a smaller trail pops out to the right, leading to the stream. Ignore it and keep straight on the main route. Around here, Geiger Grade comes into view high above. While this can be daunting—this trail meets the grade at the top—the route continues its pace clear to the top.

VIRGINIA CITY

Virginia City became the booming town it was (said to have been the most important city between Denver and San Francisco during its time) because of the Comstock Lode discovery in 1859. In its heyday of mining, this area produced more than $700 million, creating a few overnight millionaires and attracting hungry folk who had little left after visiting one of the town's one-hundred-plus saloons. These riotous conditions spurred much lore—tales that are so mixed into this town's history that sometimes it feels impossible to separate the two.

In fact, that is how the annual ostrich and camel races, a sixty-five-year tradition, came to be. It started when the city's newspaper, the *Territorial Enterprise,* wrote a fake article about camels racing in town. The unsuspecting *San Francisco Chronicle* reprinted the story, but when the Bay Area paper caught on, they took part in the fun, sending a team of jockeys and camels to Virginia City the next year to compete.

Perhaps this prank inspired the loose journalism of Mark Twain as he wrote for the very same Virginia City paper and later within his book *Roughing It*. He was known to say: "Get your facts first, and then you can distort them as much as you please," and his writing reflects that. His work regaled tales of drunken debauchery, fighting, and liberties taken with local notables.

To this day, an air of fantasy surrounds the well-preserved town. Walk past buildings from the late 1800s along the boardwalks, while hopping from the Bucket of Blood Saloon to the Silver Queen Hotel. Tour the Chollar or Ponderosa Mine, sip a drink looking out over the 100-mile view, try to communicate with ghosts, or enjoy one of the many parades and events the town hosts.

In about 0.1 mile, another trail heads to the left. Again, continue straight. When you make your descent back to the trailhead, mind this part; it is the section with the most sloped, rocky, and difficult footing. As promised, at the 1-mile mark, the trail makes two sharp turns before resuming its gentle navigation of the hillside. At 1.6 miles, after an old wooden gate appears on the right, a very convincing trail of the same width juts out directly east. Ignore it, as it ascends with a steep pitch; the Toll Road looks more level as it curves around south.

Near the trailhead, look for Owl Rock, on the ridge to the right in this photo, which attracts local climbers.

The trail continues business as usual until 2.1 miles, where a driveway comes into view on the right. This is private property, and it lines the remaining 0.7 mile of the trail. Here, the way becomes more level, smooth, and easier on the feet.

The trail concludes at Geiger Grade, which, in truth, does not make for the most satisfying ending point. Create the finish you wish here, soaking in the views and enjoying the satisfaction of climbing a mountain. Follow the trail in reverse to return to the trailhead. Remember to take care with your footing, as the loose rock makes the way unstable. It can help to walk on the shallow, flat parts as much as possible. Just take your time.

Next page: *Mount Rose Ski Tahoe resort (Slide Mountain) as seen from the trail to Church's Pond (Trail 37)*

GALENA

Southwest of Reno along Mount Rose Highway, Nevada 431, lies a small community nestled into the Sierra Nevada foothills. The area is called Galena, so named for its mineral history. Originally established in the 1860s to mine gold, its rock was found to be too rich in lead sulphide, a.k.a. galena, to be profitable. The area lived on as a prosperous timber and ore processing town before heavy snows and fires convinced residents to abandon it.

Galena's proximity to the greater Reno metropolitan area and the Mount Rose Wilderness grants it incredible access to the outdoors. Five major creeks define the landscape and direct the majority of hikes. From north to south, the creeks are Thomas, Whites, Jones, Galena, and Brown's. The water flows from the melting snowcap on Mount Rose down to Steamboat Creek, and eventually deposits into the Truckee River.

The Galena Creek Visitor Center is a great place to get your bearings. It offers free educational displays on the local environment and its dependents. Exhibits rotate regularly but include topics such as watersheds, lichen, animal tracks, regional birds, history, and more. Guided hikes, programs, and presentations are all regularly offered as well. Galena trails are most popular during the summer, when the pine forests and cool creeks provide respite from the high desert heat. During winter, Galena is a popular place to cut Christmas trees (permits available through Galena Creek Visitor Center), play in the snow, and snowshoe.

35 Lower Thomas Creek Trail

DISTANCE:	5.7 miles roundtrip
ELEVATION GAIN:	760 feet
HIGH POINT:	5965 feet
DIFFICULTY:	Moderate
FITNESS:	Walkers, hikers, runners, cyclists
FAMILY-FRIENDLY:	Yes
DOG-FRIENDLY:	Yes, leashed
AMENITIES:	Pet waste stations, benches, covered picnic tables, playground, equestrian parking
CONTACT:	Washoe County, download map from website
GPS:	39.40481°, -119.80137°
BEFORE YOU GO:	Arrowcreek Park open sunrise to sunset (hours posed at entrance gate). This is bear country; proper food and trash storage is required.

GETTING THERE

Driving: From I-580 south (US Highway 395 south), take exit 26 for Damonte Ranch Parkway. Turn right, then continue onto Arrowcreek Parkway for 3.1 miles. Turn left into the parking lot.

The Thomas Creek Trail is broken into lower and upper segments. This entry focuses on the lower segment that terminates at North Timberline Drive. The upper segment continues west from that point for 7.8 miles, to the Rim to Reno Trail (see Go Farther), which connects to Mount Rose. Users who live near this trail could walk from their house to the third-tallest mountain in the Tahoe basin, though this would demand nearly 25 miles and almost 5500 feet of elevation gain—maybe an aspiration for future adventures!

This is a nice trail with a steady grade. Lined with aspens nearly all the way up the creek, it makes a stunning stroll any time of the year, but is best March–October. Because it

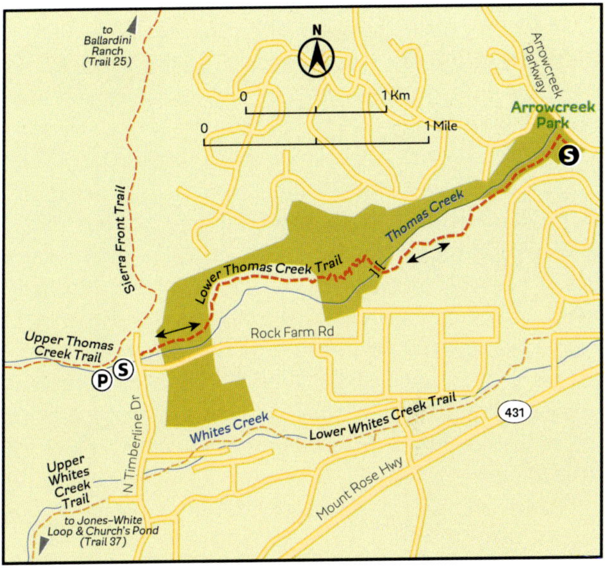

connects to a neighborhood, this is busy any time of the day, but quietest in early evening.

There is no restroom at the trailhead, but one is available at the Upper Thomas Creek trailhead on Timberline Drive.

GET MOVING

From the parking lot, walk west through the park and locate the trail at the northwestern edge (across the grassy fields). There is an equestrian trail on the northwest side of the parking lot that is a perfectly acceptable alternate start, though it will add about 300 feet each way.

The trail travels along the ambient creek and sticks to the southeast side of the water for the first 1.2 miles. Great Basin sagebrush and antelope bitterbrush line the trail, and aspens offer shade and quiet cover from the nearby neighborhood. Be sure to visit when the leaves turn golden, about mid-September through mid-October.

At 0.7 mile, the trail crosses a dirt road and is well marked on both sides. Continue straight for another 0.1 mile. At this point, the trail veers right and up onto a sagebrush-filled slope. This section diverts briefly from the creek, replacing riparian views with big vistas of Reno, the Virginia Range, and Mount Rose.

Here, social trails interrupt this official route but should be obvious enough to avoid, as they will be markedly smaller, less established, and lead toward the neighborhood or golf course. The most difficult social trail to distinguish is at 1.1 miles, where the trail forks. Keep right here to take the northern prong of this intersection. After 0.1 mile, reach the creek (a good indication you've gone the right direction!), where a footbridge carries you across. Immediately after, make a left to head west.

For 0.6 mile, the trail zigzags up a hill above the creek while heading west. This section gains 180 feet of elevation. Mount Rose, which has loomed for a while, now pops out center stage and oh so beautiful. Aspens peek out along the creek in the canyon just south of the trail, but they come into clear view around 1.8 miles. After you reach the top of the switchbacks (a dizzying total of fifteen), the trail travels just 1 mile more to the Upper Thomas Creek junction, with a total of 240 feet of elevation to gain.

In the last 0.2 mile, as the trail returns to the creek, be sure to search for springtime wildflowers, such as phlox, bristly fiddleneck, and aspen onion. The Lower Thomas Creek trail segment finishes when the trail reaches North Timberline Drive. Retrace your steps back to Arrowcreek Park, or explore one of the other trails that branch out from here.

GO FARTHER

From the western terminus of this hike, there are several options to extend your day. To continue along Upper Thomas Creek, locate the trail directly across North Timberline Drive.

From Arrowcreek Park, Mount Rose towers over aspens in winter.

It is a straight shot west and easy to follow as it gains (and gains and gains) elevation, eventually meeting with the Rim to Reno Trail, with access to Mount Rose. (Note: Bicycles are prohibited in the Mount Rose Wilderness.)

For a smaller adventure along the Upper Thomas Creek trail, trek the first 1.5 miles and turn south onto the Dry Pond Trail. This connects to the Whites Creek Trail and the greater Jones-Whites Loop. Dry Pond, which is 1.1 miles from the Thomas Creek junction, is a lovely meadow to relax in.

You could also follow the Sierra Front Trail that connects (in 5.6 miles) to Ballardini Ranch (Trail 25). Walk 450 feet north on North Timberline Drive to the Upper Thomas Creek Trail parking lot. Continue north past the lot, where there's a sign for the Sierra Front Trail toward Ballardini Ranch.

36 Lower Whites Creek Trail

DISTANCE: 7.2 miles roundtrip
ELEVATION GAIN: 950 feet
HIGH POINT: 5950 feet
DIFFICULTY: Easy to moderate
FITNESS: Walkers, hikers, runners, cyclists
FAMILY-FRIENDLY: Yes
DOG-FRIENDLY: Yes, leashed
AMENITIES: Portable restrooms, playground, picnic area
CONTACT: Washoe County, download map from website
GPS: 39.39624°, -119.78343°
BEFORE YOU GO: Open sunrise to sunset (hours posed at entrance gate). This is bear country; proper food and trash storage is required. Trail crosses three roads, some have blind spots. Creek crossings can be difficult, especially in spring and high snow years.

GETTING THERE

Driving: From I-580 south (US Highway 395 south), take exit 24 to merge onto NV 431 west. Take a right off the freeway exit to

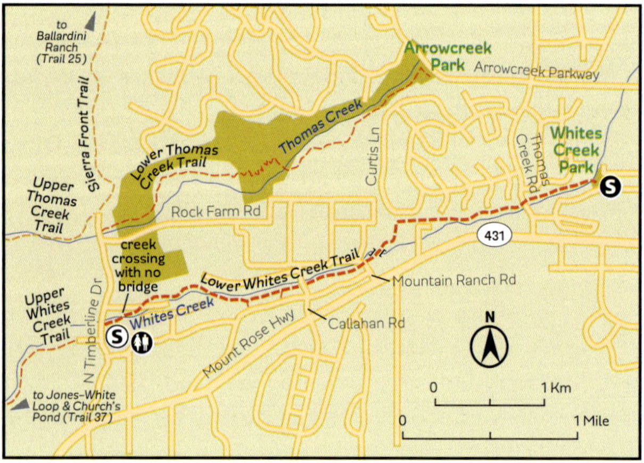

head west. In 1 mile, turn right onto Telluride Drive and continue for 0.3 mile. Turn left onto Killington Drive and continue for 0.3 mile until the road dead-ends at Whites Creek Park. Continue for 260 feet, then turn left to park in the northwesternmost part of the park.

This trail is special, maybe because of the great passion of locals who championed the creation of this trail system in the 1990s. To this day, it remains a very popular route during the snow-free months. Though it is at a higher elevation and follows a creek, there are exposed sections, so bring plenty of water and protect your skin from the sun. Late spring (May and June) is the best time to visit, as temperatures remain tolerable and flowers, like Palmer's penstemon, firecracker penstemon, great mullein, and even California poppy, are in full bloom. Note that the trail crosses several roads, some of which have blind spots. Also, creek crossings can be difficult in spring and high snow years.

GET MOVING

Locate the trail, marked with three granite boulders and a sign, in the northwest corner of the parking lot. The picnic tables and well-tread areas near the creek can make getting started a little confusing. To stay on track, keep to the leftmost trail (west). Once oriented, relax and take in the murmur and views from the creek, along with the refreshing shade (spring to fall) from aspens that seem to touch the sky.

At 0.2 mile, the trail makes a sharp right to cross the creek. A different trail continues straight, which makes this intersection tricky. To stay on the official trail, watch for this sharp right. Just 50 feet later, find a small footbridge to cross the creek. On the other side, take the trail leading west (ignore the one that splits right and leads to the neighborhood). Periodic social trails like this connect to the neighborhoods; only the tricky ones will be mentioned here.

Aspens shine bright green in spring along Lower Whites Creek. From April to October, these trees create a beautiful canopy on this trail.

Though the trail follows the creek for the first mile, plants like desert peach, antelope bitterbrush, and poppies decorate the north side. At 0.5 mile, reach the winding Thomas Creek Road. It is difficult to see oncoming traffic, and there is no crosswalk or pedestrian light; use extreme caution crossing here. The trail picks up directly across the road.

At 1 mile, the trail diverts from the creek, and a fence marking private property takes its place. Sounds from the road seep into your surroundings as the foliage opens up to a sagebrush-dominant landscape. This section might feel a bit mundane compared to the lush environment you just left. If you don't appreciate this stretch, it's a quick 0.6-mile jog to where the trail meets back up to the creek.

Before that, though, at 1.1 miles, come to a private road marked with No Trespassing signs. Take in the incredible views of Mount Rose and Slide Mountain here as the trail wraps around the north side of the road. The trail continues for another 0.2 mile to another easily missed intersection. Make a sharp left here and head south for about 600 feet before the trail makes a couple of turns as it approaches the creek.

At 1.6 miles, cross the creek with the aid of a sturdy bridge, then head up wooden stairs that lead south. Another trail, created either by or for mountain bikers, avoids the stairs. Both lead to the same place. The trail crosses Mountain Ranch Road at 1.8 miles. It's a lot slower and quieter, but still take caution because (again) there is no crosswalk, no light, and blind turns in both directions, with visibility of about 50 feet.

On the other side, the trail opens up to a wide dirt area, allowing access to the creek. Keep to the left (south) side to relocate the trail, though it is fairly inconsequential if you follow a wrong one here, since every option eventually funnels together. At 2.1 miles, cross Callahan Road. This one feels safest yet, with a crosswalk and ample visibility. The crosswalk does not lead directly to the trail, so on the other side, head north about 20 feet to find it again.

When the giraffe-like aspens resume their post along the creek at 2.5 miles, feel relief in the brief pockets of shade as the trail undulates along the creek for the next 0.8 mile. The final road crossing comes at 3.3 miles. It is a quiet but overgrown intersection on a private dirt road. Thriving plants sometimes obscure the trail entrance on the other side, even though it is directly across. After this road crossing, pines begin to pepper the environment.

At 3.4 miles, the trail crosses the creek, but there is no bridge. It can be dangerous here when the water is high. Be extremely careful, and know that it's always better to get your feet wet than to step on a slippery rock and fall. There is never any shame in turning around, either.

After the crossing, it is only 0.2 mile to North Timberline Drive. Over this distance, the trail travels closer to private residences. From the road, there are many options to continue your hike (see Go Farther). To return to the trailhead, make the same journey in reverse. On the way back, beautiful aspens frame the stunning views of the Virginia Range.

GO FARTHER

North Timberline Drive offers several options for further adventure. A half-mile walk north on the road leads to the Lower Thomas Creek Trail (Trail 35).

Another option is to continue along Upper Whites Creek. Locate the trailhead by walking 430 feet south on the road. Look for trail signs on the road's north side that point to Whites Creek trailhead and Thomas Creek trailer parking, and follow the dirt road heading west. After 600 feet, pick up the dirt trail on the south side of the road. In 0.7 mile, reach the official trailhead. After half a mile, the trail morphs into the Church's Pond Trail (Trail 37).

37 Church's Pond

DISTANCE:	6.6 miles roundtrip
ELEVATION GAIN:	2170 feet
HIGH POINT:	8350 feet
DIFFICULTY:	Challenging
FITNESS:	Walkers, hikers, runners
FAMILY-FRIENDLY:	Yes, but steep sections may be too challenging for young ones. See Go Farther section for more suitable options.
DOG-FRIENDLY:	Yes, leashed for first mile only
AMENITIES:	Benches, restrooms
CONTACT:	Washoe County, download map from website or get at Galena Creek Visitor Center
GPS:	39.361771°, -119.857259°
BEFORE YOU GO:	Open sunrise to sunset (hours posted at entrance gate). This is bear country; proper food and trash storage is required.

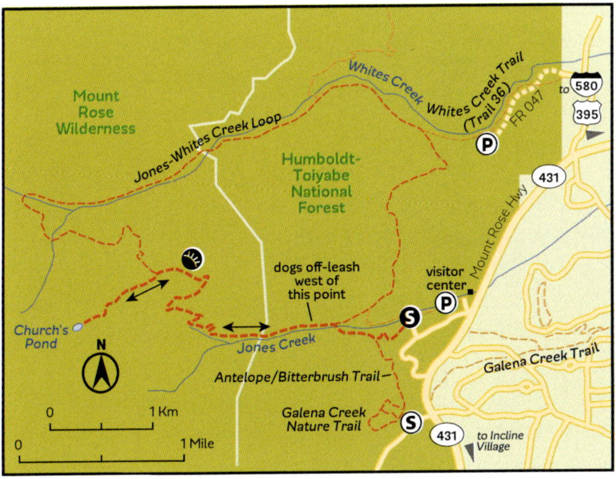

Looking west up to Mount Rose from the top of the climb to Church's Pond, a great place to stop and take in the 365-degree vistas

GETTING THERE

Driving: From I-580 south (US Highway 395 south), take exit 24 for NV 431 west toward North Lake Tahoe. Turn right onto NV 431 (Mount Rose Highway). Continue for 5.8 miles, then turn right toward Galena Creek Visitor Center. Continue 0.4 mile and park in the third parking lot.

There's no need to sugarcoat it; this hike is challenging—one of the steepest ascents in this book—with unrelenting uphill sections (though the navigation and footing are fine). But it is highlighted for a reason: fantastic views of the Mount Rose Wilderness and Truckee Meadows await, along with beautiful spring wildflowers, golden fall aspens, and a grand sense of accomplishment. This trail leads to the highest point in the book, giving a real flavor of a Tahoe Basin adventure without driving up a hill or battling for parking among throngs of tourists.

The best time to visit is early June through October, but winter trekkers can enjoy a quiet snowshoeing adventure.

Because it is a bit cooler and partially shaded, it is very popular on weekends during summer. Note that bicycles are prohibited west of Jones Creek crossing.

GET MOVING

Locate the trailhead at the northwest corner of the Jones Creek trailhead parking lot (in the dirt trailer parking area). The trail is a wide, lovely, sandy path. However, keep an eye out for rocks sticking up from the trail.

At 0.3 mile, reach a marked intersection. Continue right here, as the trail transitions from sagebrush to forest. At 0.6 mile, cross Jones Creek and come to another trail intersection. Here marks the point where the 9.2-mile Jones-Whites loop joins together, which is why trail signs point right (east) for the Jones-Whites trail. Ignore this and continue to the left (west) along the loop toward Church's Pond.

Here is where the uphill fun begins. Pace yourself over the next 2.5 miles as the trail ascends 250 feet every 0.3 mile (on average). Take breaks as needed and don't berate yourself—this is a very strenuous pitch even for advanced hikers.

Try to distract yourself from the rude slant of the trail by taking in the area's flora, like the purple flowers of the aptly named mahala mat that show through July. Snowbrush ceanothus and curl leaf mountain mahogany are common, as are the rust-colored stalks of woodland pinedrops. Bright red snowplants might surprise you within the monotonous browns of dirt and bark. As the elevation sweeps up, paintbrush, lupine, and daggerpod disperse across the landscape. Aspens, during fall especially, show off along Jones Creek.

At 0.9 mile, dogs are allowed to continue their journey west off-leash, though on weekends, this trail is very popular, and dogs should remain under strict voice control at all times. When it is quieter here, too, bears are commonly sighted, a good excuse to keep your pups close. The trail approaches the boundary of the Mount Rose Wilderness 0.1 mile after this milestone.

At 1.4 miles (650 feet of gain from the Jones Creek intersection), reach the first of six switchbacks. The second to last switchback comes at 2 miles, after another 400 feet of gain. This is the longest switchback, but one of the most rewarding, as about halfway through its 0.3-mile, 310-foot climb are incredible views of the ski runs on the north side of Slide Mountain and Washoe Valley.

The trail continues another 0.3 mile and 240 feet before leveling out at the ridge, where it opens and reveals the beauty of this wilderness. Take a moment to pause and congratulate yourself before continuing on to the pond. Here, there is a social trail that leads to the east (right) for a nice place to sit and rest, and to the west (left) to connect to the Jones-Whites Creek Loop junction.

At 2.7 miles, just 0.1 mile down the trail, is the official intersection for the Jones-Whites Creek Loop, which heads north to complete its 9-mile journey. This intersection is marked. If you are interested in continuing this way, see Go Farther. Otherwise, continue straight (west) to Church's Pond. The next 0.6 mile is the last uphill section, about 260 feet. At 3.3 miles, arrive at Church's Pond. When you're ready, retrace your steps to the trailhead—it's all downhill from here!

GO FARTHER

The complete Jones-Whites Creek Loop is a beautiful trail, with a total length of 9.3 miles. It descends from 8085 feet (its highest point, at the trail intersection with Church's Pond) down to 6020 feet across 6.7 miles. Hike counterclockwise from the Jones Creek intersection to save yourself the hassle of the strenuous uphill described in the Church's Pond approach.

A family-friendly option from the Jones Creek trailhead is the 0.7-mile Galena Creek Nature Trail loop. To access it, start at the trailhead for the main trail and travel 0.3 mile. Turn left at the intersection and walk 0.2 mile along the Jones-Whites Creek Loop trail to the Jones-Whites Creek Loop trailhead parking lot,

Crossing Brown's Creek on a footbridge

where the Antelope Bitterbrush Trail starts. From here, walk 0.4 mile and make the first right onto the Nature Trail. Enjoy information on local ecology and history (pick up a brochure at the Galena Creek Visitor Center). When you've completed the loop, turn left back onto the Antelope Bitterbrush Trail and follow it back to the Jones Creek trailhead parking lot.

38 Brown's Creek Trail

DISTANCE: 5.2-mile loop
ELEVATION GAIN: 1010 feet
HIGH POINT: 6280 feet
DIFFICULTY: Moderate to challenging
FITNESS: Walkers, hikers, runners, cyclists
FAMILY-FRIENDLY: Yes
DOG-FRIENDLY: Yes, leashed
AMENITIES: Pet waste stations, trash cans
CONTACT: Washoe County, download map from website
GPS: 39.34911°, -119.83278°
BEFORE YOU GO: This is bear country; proper food and trash storage is required.

GETTING THERE

Driving: From I-580 south (US Highway 395 south), take exit 24 and merge onto NV 431 (Mount Rose Highway) west. Turn

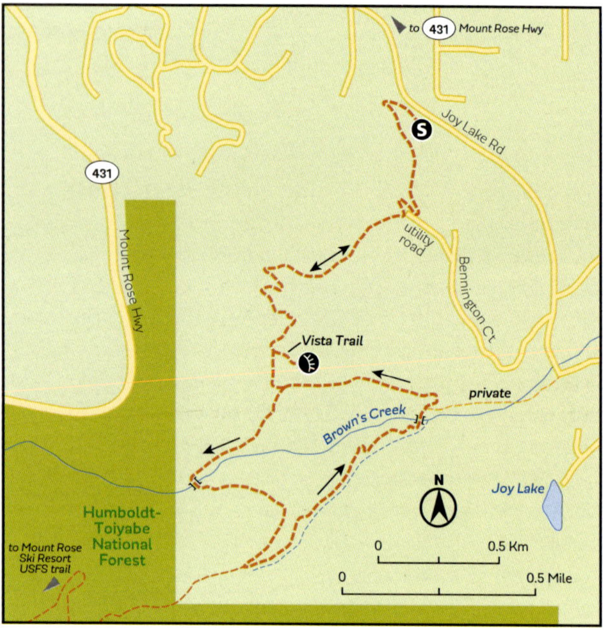

right off the freeway exit and continue along the highway for 5.9 miles. Turn left onto Joy Lake Road and continue for 1.5 miles. The trailhead parking is on the left.

One of the many creeks fanning from the greater Mount Rose area, Brown's Creek is another stunning example of the eastern edge of the Sierra Nevada. Exposed and rocky, this trail can be difficult, but it rewards with views and peaceful creeks. Don't assume that pine trees along the trail will provide shade or that higher elevation will be an easier environment to walk through; bring proper sun protection and plenty of water.

This trail keeps you on your toes. It gains more than 1000 feet, but also loses nearly half that, meaning trail users alternate between gaining and losing elevation the entire trip. It is a good workout if nothing else. Visiting is best during spring and fall, but the trail sees plenty of use year-round.

GET MOVING

Locate the trailhead across the street from the parking lot, marked with a large sign. Almost immediately, the trail nears private property, a common occurrence on this trail. Be respectful; keep dogs on leash and children close.

Continue up the trail—and it will be *up*, about 230 feet of elevation gain in the first 0.5 mile. Appreciate the refreshing shade from Jeffrey pines. Their faint vanilla-butterscotch scent might snag your attention, along with the "cheeseburger" song of chickadees. While you enjoy the Sierra foliage, be sure to watch your feet; this trail is full of exposed rocks.

Unlike many trails in this book, this one is easy to follow, with no other trails interrupting the first 2 miles. This luxury allows you to sink even deeper into the peace of the forest. Around 0.3 mile, the canopy opens and reveals stunning views to the east. The arched Galena Creek bridge on US Highway 395 makes for a beautiful sight here, with the Virginia Range behind it. (The bridge is an even more stunning attraction when driving through Washoe Valley, where it frames the height of the Carson Range behind it.)

At 0.5 mile, the trail reaches another private property sign, marked with a large fence and water tower. About 50 feet later is a private access road. The trail picks up across the road, slightly to the left and marked with a sign. When on the trail again, look immediately right to the first view of Slide Mountain.

Continue along this first ascent (yes, first) for the next 0.9 mile and 330 feet of elevation gain. Here, on the left (southeast) of the trail, is the Vista Trail junction. Take this now, as it is flat and a welcome reward for completing this climb. The viewpoint looks out over the mountain valleys between here and Washoe Lake. In spring and fall, when the mountains still have snow, you can pick out the high peaks of the Pine Nut

Mountains, a range that skirts the southeastern border of the Eagle and Carson Valleys. Slide Mountain is easily identified to the west.

Return to the main trail and turn left (south), which is downhill—for now. In 600 feet, come to the loop. Turn right to head west. This section is exposed but offers a lovely view of Slide Mountain. Hear the sound of Brown's Creek at 1.8 miles, and watch the water to see a small cascade or two rushing eastward toward Steamboat Creek, which the trail meets at 2 miles. Here, follow the switchback down to the footbridge over the water, not the trail that continues west.

After enjoying the water, continue. Another switchback appears at 2.5 miles, marked with a sign directing Brown's Creek Trail users to the left. As with the last switchback, another trail travels west from this point, entering Forest Service land. Turn left and emerge almost level with another smaller creek surrounded by aspen trees. Follow this creek, enjoying the sounds of rushing water and chirping birds, along with flowers like mule ears, heart-leaf milkweed, and mahala mat.

At 3.2 miles, cross Brown's Creek once again. Pause and soak in the idyllic scene, including miniature waterfalls and ample shade, because the next section is difficult. A private property sign, near the Brown's Creek bridge, marks the start of the last uphill stretch, about 380 feet in 0.6 mile. With gorgeous views of the ski resort beckoning you through this difficult section, return to the loop split. A sign marks the direction back to the trailhead. Head straight and let this (mostly) downhill trail take you back to the parking lot.

GO FARTHER

The Galena Creek Trail is a wonderful way to extend this hike. To access it, drive west on Joy Lake Road, toward the Mount Rose Highway. About 0.4 mile before Mount Rose Highway (the first right after Pine Creek Road) is access to the trail. This is about the midpoint of the trail. Take a right to head east and

Looking up at Mount Rose Ski Resort (also known as Slide Mountain)

follow the creek on its descent to Phillip and Annie Callahan Park, about 1.6 miles with a 500-foot descent (one-way). Or turn left from the trailhead to head west along the trail as it wraps around to Douglas Fir Drive, about 0.8 mile and 250 feet of elevation gain (one-way). Either way, enjoy gorgeous Galena Creek, towering pines, and quaking aspens.

Next page: *Surrounded by gorgeous red rocks, the gazebo at the high point on Deadman's Creek Trail (Trail 42) offers spectacular views of Washoe Lake.*

WASHOE VALLEY

The Washoe (Wá·šiw) are the "people from here" and the namesake of the valley and lake just south of Reno. Lake Tahoe (Da ow aga) was at the center of Washoe ancestral land. Summers were spent at the lake, and winters spent in the lower valleys of present-day Nevada. The Washoe have lived in this area for at least 6000 years, and the environment is deeply integrated into their traditions and cultures.

Spring was an important time; when warm enough, the first journeys to Lake Tahoe would occur. Deep knowledge of local flora was passed from generation to generation, a skill needed to gather plants that have a short life in our harsh environment. Pinyon pine nuts (ťágɨms) were a nutritious source of food—a reason why the pinyon is Nevada's state tree. The Washoe caught game and Lahontan cutthroat trout and wove baskets using cattails and willows from around Washoe Lake. During the fall, great rabbit drives took place to gather meat and pelts for the upcoming winter.

This routine was destroyed by emigrants moving onto the land and settling within the Truckee Meadows. Through the hardships the Washoe people have faced, including the depletion of resources like pinyon trees and cutthroat trout, they have survived and still call the valleys below the Sierra Nevada home.

39 Davis Creek Park

DISTANCE: 2.1-mile loop
ELEVATION GAIN: 260 feet
HIGH POINT: 5310 feet
DIFFICULTY: Easy
FITNESS: Walkers, hikers, runners, cyclists
FAMILY-FRIENDLY: Yes
DOG-FRIENDLY: Yes, leashed
AMENITIES: Pet waste stations, restrooms, benches, picnic areas, fishing pond, equestrian-friendly parking
CONTACT: Washoe County, download map from website
GPS: 39.303610°, –119.833274°
BEFORE YOU GO: Day-use parking is open sunrise to sunset. Permits are required to fish, and reservations are required for camping. This is bear country; proper food and trash storage is required.

GETTING THERE

Driving: From I-580 south (US Highway 395 south), take exit 16 for US 395 ALT and turn right. After 450 feet, make the first right onto Davis Creek Campground Road. Continue for 0.3 mile, then turn left onto Davis Creek Picnic Road. Turn left after 0.2 mile, at the sign for nature trail parking. Find the small lot on the left 160 feet after this junction.

Nestled between Slide Mountain and Washoe Lake, Davis Creek Park is surrounded by the sweet-smelling pines of the Carson Range. Enjoy both mountain and high desert landscapes, along with a history of Thoroughbred horses, ranching, logging, and ice production. Find a list of events on the Washoe County website (see Resources).

Today, Davis Creek Park protects its natural beauty, rather than extracts it. Here, find lovely campsites and trails. Undulating, soft tread gives users a taste of hiking the Sierra Nevada without demanding much time or effort. You can feel the sense

The Nature Trail in Davis Creek Park starts in a tranquil setting.

of adventure at water crossings strewn with wildflowers, in skies dotted with eagles and osprey, and in elevation gain that gets the heart pumping. In this way, this loop makes for a great family outing, especially in summer.

GET MOVING

The Davis Creek Park Loop combines the 0.7-mile Nature Trail with the 1.7-mile Discovery Loop to create a 2.1-mile super loop around the park.

From the Nature Trail parking area, locate the trailhead on the eastern side of the lot. The trail starts on the northern side of the road and is marked by a large sign. Before heading

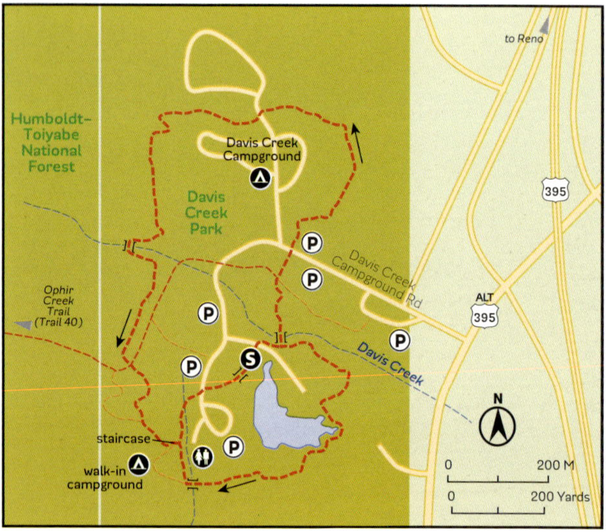

out, pause at the interpretive sign to pick up a guide, which explains points of interest at numbered posts along the trail. This is a great way to learn about the natural environment.

About 150 feet into the trail, it dead-ends at a north-south trail. A sign points to the Discovery Trail to the left (north) and the Nature Trail to the right (south). Continue right to stay on the Nature Trail. Cross the bridge and keep to the left. The trail wraps around east, revealing views of the pond, with Slide Mountain towering above. This is a lovely section, popular with anglers and families. The trail is a bit rocky, so watch your footing.

At 0.5 mile, cross a small creek over an equally small bridge before turning right to head north. A sneaky social trail might lure you to the south, but ignore it. The lovely vanilla-butterscotch scent of Jeffrey pines sometimes wafts here. If you come to a tree with giant fissures, sniff between the bark. Look lower, too, because western columbines grow along the water here in late June.

THE WASHOE ZEPHYR

Mark Twain wrote of the Washoe Zephyr in *Roughing It*—which is his painted "experience" of life in early Nevada just before it gained statehood: "But seriously a Washoe wind is by no means a trifling matter. It blows flimsy houses down, lifts shingle roofs occasionally, rolls up tin ones like sheet music, now and then blows a stage coach over and spills the passengers; and tradition says the reason there are so many bald people there, is, that the wind blows the hair off their heads while they are looking skyward after their hats."

Twain was known for his embellished Nevada stories, but his account of the local zephyr is not far from the truth. This wind is a daily occurrence during the warmer months, usually escorting the afternoon into evening. It's caused by rising heat from the valleys mixed with cooling air over the Sierra, plus increased velocity as it races downslope. Wind speeds of 20 to 30 miles an hour are common—and usually welcomed as a natural air conditioner, cooling 95-degree days into temperate evenings.

The Washoe Zephyr can seem mild compared to other wind events that speckle our local weather. Gusts in Washoe Valley have reached more than 90 miles per hour, and serious windstorms have been known to topple eighteen-wheelers onto their sides as they drive through the valley along US Highway 395. Summiting peaks like the one on Deadman's Creek Trail (Trail 42) can highlight the power (and often annoyance) of the wind. Don't let it stop you, though—just don't look up for your missing hat, or you may come home hairless.

Find a wooden staircase extending east-west after 0.1 mile. There will be signs for the Discovery Trail here. Instead of climbing the stairs, continue along the lovely creek for another 430 feet, as the trail curves east and comes to a road crossing. On the other side of the road, notice how soft and sandy the trail becomes. About 150 feet from the road, the trail comes to a Y; make a left here to cross the bridge and continue on the trail. Soon after, the trail makes another Y. Again, take the left arm to stay on the trail. The opposite segments of both Ys meet with the pond, and you will probably see people walking these trails to reach the shoreline.

A quaint bridge near the trailhead is surrounded by lush greenery.

The trail meets back at a road at 0.7 mile, across the street from the trailhead. From here, repeat the same steps to cross the road and reach the trail junction. This time, turn left (north) to take the Discovery Trail. At 0.8 mile, the trail comes to an intersection with the Ophir Creek Trail (Trail 40). This junction makes a sort of X. Take the top right (northeastern) leg. A lower right turn will land you at the equestrian parking and trailhead for Ophir Creek.

The trail soon crosses Davis Creek Campground Road and resumes along a parking lot. After this road crossing, travel through classic Great Basin sagebrush country for 0.3 mile. Exceptional antelope bitterbrush towers as tall as trees here, standing about 8 feet high. Around early May, look for Brown's peonies. In June, keep an eye out for the white flowers of the branching phacelia and the purple flowers of the silvery lupine.

At 1.1 miles, cross another road. The two sides of the trail don't match up exactly, but they are well marked. Over the next 0.3 mile, the trail gains about 120 feet of elevation. Continue westward, traveling along a dry creek speckled with aspen and other water-loving plants, accompanied by the signature summertime smell of grilled hot dogs and sunscreen. A few social trails lead to picnic areas on the north side of the dry pond, but avoid them to stay on track.

The trail curves to the south at 1.3 miles, where a sign shows the correct route. Here, it looks much different than it did at the beginning; the pine understory is practically nonexistent, revealing the lower edges of the Sierra Nevada landscape. At the height of the climb (at 1.4 miles), the trail switches back and begins to descend into a second creek canyon. At 1.5 miles, reach a bridge over the creek, a pleasant place to dip your hands into the cool water and enjoy the Woods' rose in early spring, or later in the season, wildflowers like western columbine.

At 1.7 miles, come to another well-marked junction with the Ophir Creek Trail. Stay to the left to remain on the Discovery Trail. In 0.1 mile, the trail meets at familiar wooden steps leading down to the Nature Trail. Descend the handful of stairs, then turn left to retrace your steps 0.2 mile back to the trailhead.

GO FARTHER

An easy way to extend a hike within Davis Creek Regional Park is to explore Ophir Creek Trail (Trail 40). Please note that it is much more demanding than the park loop. Though challenging, it rewards users with a beautiful creekside spot to enjoy mountain views. There are several ways to access it, the easiest of which is heading left (west) on the wooden staircase 1.8 miles into the park loop trail.

40 Ophir Creek Trail

DISTANCE:	4.4 miles roundtrip
ELEVATION GAIN:	1060 feet
HIGH POINT:	6100 feet
DIFFICULTY:	Challenging
FITNESS:	Walkers, hikers, runners, cyclists
FAMILY-FRIENDLY:	Yes, but steep sections might be difficult for young children.
DOG-FRIENDLY:	Yes, leashed
AMENITIES:	Pet waste stations, benches
CONTACT:	Washoe County, download map from website
GPS:	39.30235°, -119.83396°
BEFORE YOU GO:	Day-use parking is open sunrise to sunset. Permits are required to fish, and reservations are required for camping. This is bear country; proper food and trash storage is required.

GETTING THERE

Driving: From I-580 south (US Highway 395 south), use exit 16 for US 395 ALT and turn right. After 450 feet, make the first right onto Davis Creek Campground Road. Continue for 0.3

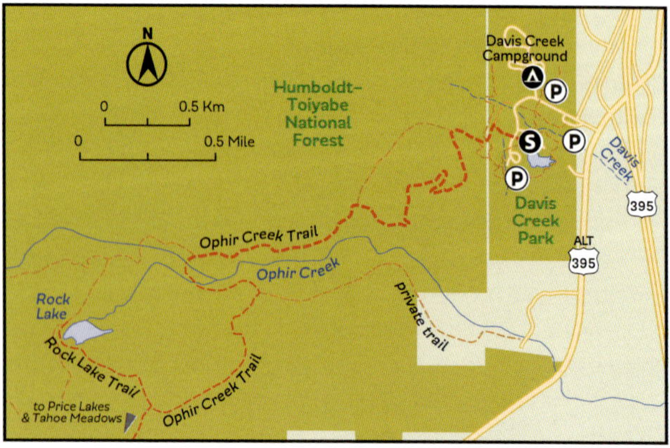

mile, then turn left onto Davis Creek Picnic Road. Take this for another 0.3 mile and park where the road ends.

The Ophir Creek Trail is filled with majestic firs and sweet-smelling Jeffrey pines and has a luxuriously soft trail as it follows its namesake along the south side of Slide Mountain (see the "Mount Rose vs. Mount Rose" sidebar in Trail 42 for more information). The section is just a portion of the full 7.5-mile roundtrip trail that leads to Tahoe Meadows along the Mount Rose Highway (a fantastic place to spot wildflowers!). Borrowing from biblical origins, Ophir is aptly named; its rich scenery is not one to miss, especially in spring when the creek, in all its glorious cascades, flows at peak height.

The best time to hike Ophir Creek is spring through fall, as snow is likely during winter. Weekends during warmer months can be busy.

GET MOVING

From the parking lot circle at the end of Davis Creek Picnic Road, locate the trailhead on the southwest side of the lot, by the restroom. The trail immediately begins to gain elevation, about 100 feet in the 0.2 mile before the Ophir Creek Trail splits off to the west. At this intersection, marked with trail signs, turn left to continue along the Ophir Creek Trail. Though the elevation can be challenging at times, the shade, trickling creek, and sweet vanilla-butterscotch scent of the towering Jeffrey pines offer a nice incentive to keep going.

At 0.3 mile (and 70 feet of elevation gain later), the trail comes to a small creek crossing, which is easy enough to hop over, and another trail junction. This junction is marked, directing folks to take a left (heading south). Turn left here, unless you want to make up for a missed spin class at the gym. A wayward right would lead to a very challenging uphill section, though it would cut off some mileage.

Continue south. Over the next 0.5 mile, the trail gains another 200 feet as it switches back a couple of times up the mountain. This exposed section bleeds into the next 0.5 mile, which gains 270 feet of elevation. Not to worry—your lungs and thighs will get respite at 1.3 miles, where the trail begins to flatten out. Soon, the aforementioned steep trail that split off 0.3 mile back appears on the right. If a hiker approaches from this direction, congratulate them on their grand accomplishments and pat yourself on the back for making wiser choices.

After this potential interaction, look southwest down the trail. It splits into a Y here; take the right tendril of this trail split and continue to a pleasant 0.3-mile stroll. Be sure to slow down around 1.5 miles to hear the creek's growing symphony. Keep an eye out to the left (south) for an obvious place to step off the trail and view the fountain of water descending into the valley. And don't forget to look eastward; from this vista, a slice of Washoe Lake is visible between the trees.

As the trail continues, it undulates between steep and flat sections, not staying very long in either (though the steep sections always seem to tick by, while the flat parts fly). The trail reaches the pinnacle of this hike—a whopping 990 feet—at 2.1 miles. Here, the trail is escorted to the creekside by giant granite boulders. Lining the trail, these rocks show the forces of nature and offer a clue about why Slide Mountain is so named. Follow the trail until it reaches the stream, find a beautiful spot to take a rest, and catch your breath.

As you descend back to the trailhead, the flowers and finer sounds of the trail come into focus. Search for snowplants, paintbrush, and phlox, as well as the familiar "cheeseburger" call of chickadees.

GO FARTHER

Take this trail to Rock Lake, Lower and Upper Price Lakes, or all the way to Tahoe Meadows beneath Mount Rose. However, be prepared for an arduous ascent! Bring plenty of water (preferably

Granite surrounds Ophir Creek.

with electrolytes) and snacks, and take ample breaks. To start, cross the creek carefully, and only if it seems safe.

For Rock Lake: In 1 mile and 630 feet of elevation gain, turn right on the trail that heads northwest, and follow it to the lake.

For the Price Lakes: At the Rock Lake turnoff, continue left along Ophir Creek Trail for another 0.9 mile and 550 feet of elevation gain, where it turns into Country Road 315. Follow this straight north to the lakes, for 2.7 additional miles and 1400 feet of gain one-way.

For Tahoe Meadows: Follow Country Road 315 for 0.2 mile. Take a sharp left west to Tahoe Meadows, where it meets the Tahoe Rim Trail. This adds an additional 5.4 miles and 2740 feet of elevation one-way.

41 Dune Trek

DISTANCE:	5.6 miles roundtrip
ELEVATION GAIN:	250 feet
HIGH POINT:	5070 feet
DIFFICULTY:	Challenging
FITNESS:	Walkers, hikers
FAMILY-FRIENDLY:	No, surface tread and navigation can be difficult.
DOG-FRIENDLY:	Yes, leashed when within 200 feet of camping or picnic area
AMENITIES:	Pet waste stations, benches, restrooms
CONTACT:	Nevada State Parks, download map from website
GPS:	39.24783°, -119.75825°
BEFORE YOU GO:	Entrance fee is required. Self-pay station at the north parking lot accepts cash only; main entrance accepts cards. Park is open sunrise to sunset.

GETTING THERE

Driving: From I-580 south (US Highway 395 south), take exit 10 for Eastlake Boulevard. Turn left onto Eastlake and continue for 3.3 miles. Turn left at the state park entrance. In 315 feet, go left again, following signs for the campground and equestrian area for 0.4 mile. Turn right into the equestrian parking lot when the road dead-ends. Signs say Equestrian Parking Only, but park rangers have confirmed that day users can park here as well.

Though a bit of a drive from Reno, Washoe Lake State Park is a gem, and wild horses are often seen here. Situated in a narrow valley between the Carson and Virginia Ranges, its main feature is Washoe Lake. The dunes along the lake's eastern shore were formed by natural events over thousands of years, with layer after layer of eroded sediment being added until they reached their current height of 30 feet.

This trail is rated challenging because of the difficult navigation. Since this is a sand trail in a land constantly manipulated

by wind, it is difficult to clearly define a path. The best practice is to bring navigation and backtrack to look for the trail again if you get lost. Signs are posted every quarter mile or so and are intended to be seen from the previous sign, though this is not always the case. To protect your eyes, wear glasses or eye protection on windy days.

GET MOVING

Finding the start of this hike can be a little challenging. The Dune Trek technically starts 0.4 mile west of the parking lot and is accessed via the South Loop. To access the trailhead, locate the smaller parking circle that leads to a corral. The trail begins in this smaller lot; it is wide and heads directly west toward the lake.

Sand dune views looking east

Immediately, the views of Mount Rose and Slide Mountain are breathtaking. A sea of sage extends on either side of the trail and, more likely than not, wild horses will be grazing on the foliage. Continue on this path for 0.4 mile, ignoring the one forking south at 0.2 mile.

Right before the official Dune Trek begins, the South Loop diverts north. Look west toward the lake to spot the Dune Trek sign to navigate to the correct trail, which commences with soft sand underfoot. It is both lovely and challenging, using different muscles than when walking on packed tread.

The first 0.5 mile travels around ponds. Here, social trails pop out and cause confusion. The trail goes along the east side of the first pond and the west of the second pond, and then makes a sharp left turn (west) on the southern shore of the third. Water in these ponds depends on seasonal precipitation, but the depression of each should be obvious even in dry years. When water is present, this is a great place to spot shorebirds like the American avocet, snowy egret, and killdeer. In fact, within the park, more than two hundred species of bird have been cataloged.

About 300 feet west of the final pond, the trail turns right to head north. Climb a small dune to complete the first mile of the trek. From the top, the trail marker should be visible on top of the next dune. The trail stays more or less straight for the next 0.4 mile. Then, at 1.4 miles, it comes to another set of small ponds. In high water years, the normal route through here becomes impassable. A trail jutting out east might seduce you to follow it, but it accesses the North Loop. Remain northbound here as much as you can. The trail mirrors the previous pattern around the ponds: staying east of the first pond, then west of the second pond.

After navigating around the second pond, a trail marker should come into view at the top of the next dune. Another northeast trail leaves from the second pond, again providing access to the North Loop. Continue straight, keeping your path in line with the upcoming trail sign. The way continues straight-ish until the 2-mile mark. Here, it heads briefly east before looping back around to the west. Intercepting this semicircle is—yes, you guessed it—another eastbound trail leading to the North Loop. Keep a keen eye west toward the top of the next dune to help orient yourself. The rhythm of the trail should breeze you through the next 0.4 mile (though nothing is guaranteed with this trail). At 2.4 miles, the dunes begin to give way to flatter ground. The trail snakes along, veering east, then west, then back east, finally straightening out as it intersects another eastbound trail.

In the final 0.2 mile, it becomes very convoluted. At 2.8 miles, the trail reaches a large intersection. Make a sharp left toward the lake here and reward yourself with a relaxing sit at the water. Take the same(ish) path back, or take the Beach Stroll 2.1 miles south to the start of the Dune Trek.

GO FARTHER

Continue your exploration of the state park. The North, East, and South Loops are fair options, though they seem more suited to equestrians or cyclists. A great option is the Deadman's Creek Trail (Trail 42). To access it, walk about 500 feet back along the road from the parking lot toward the visitor center. Cross Eastlake Boulevard and continue southeast past the visitor center. Take the trail here that parallels Eastlake for 0.6 mile before dead-ending at the Deadman's Creek trailhead, where you will start the hike. In total, this journey will add 2.7 miles and around 320 feet of elevation gain.

42 Deadman's Creek Trail

DISTANCE:	1.2-mile loop
ELEVATION GAIN:	290 feet
HIGH POINT:	5370 feet
DIFFICULTY:	Moderate
FITNESS:	Walkers, hikers, runners
FAMILY-FRIENDLY:	Yes
DOG-FRIENDLY:	Yes, leashed
AMENITIES:	Pet waste station, benches; more amenities at park entrance to the north
CONTACT:	Nevada State Parks, download map from website
GPS:	39.238357°, -119.766511°
BEFORE YOU GO:	Expect wild horses and other high desert animals and reptiles. Adjacent trails are popular OHV routes; expect dirt bikes, cars, and other off-road vehicles nearby.

GETTING THERE

Driving: From I-580 south (US Highway 395 south), drive south out of Reno and take exit 10 for Eastlake Boulevard. Turn left off the freeway onto Eastlake. Continue for 3 miles, then locate the parking lot—a dirt turnout marked with trail signs—on the right (south) side of the road. This can be easy to miss; if you reach the Washoe Lake State Park entrance, turn around and head back south 0.3 mile.

What looks plain at first is actually a wetland paradise surrounded by stunning scenery. Deadman's Creek Trail is one of the best in this book for watching the sunset, as golden rays drag along Washoe Lake and trickle behind Mount Rose. Despite the almost-daily harrowing winds here, the trail is full of life, a testament to the strength and resilience of high-desert flora. Though short, this little trail packs beauty into each foot.

Every season here has its magic, but spring is the best time to visit, when it feels like a resplendent cove with enough nourishment for the rest of the desiccated land. Wildflowers, even the rare Carson monkeyflower, spring up. Shimmering, bright green aspen leaves contrast against a backdrop of rusty-red rock. And at the peak, a gazebo somehow withstands the fierce weather, framing Mount Rose over Washoe Lake. In springtime, all the land's features collide: high water, healthy blooms, the snowcapped Sierra, and dramatic storm clouds transforming to pink at the end of the day.

GET MOVING

From the trailhead parking lot, locate the green gate at the start of the trail. Almost immediately, the trail follows the creek, diving directly into the oasis of the canyon. After the first 100

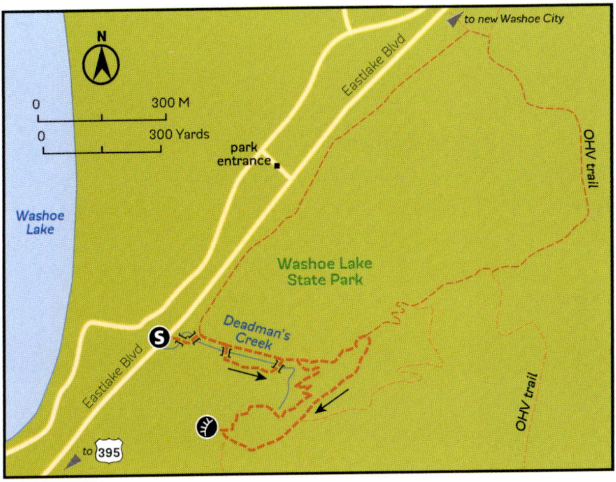

feet or so, cross the creek, which takes nothing more than a wide step over the water. On the other side, the trail begins its first climb. This is a short push—only about 40 feet of elevation gain—and is quickly over.

At 0.1 mile, the trail splits. Follow the path on the right, which takes you into the depths of the creek habitat to see beautiful foliage, find some shade, and enjoy the trickling of water. In about 120 feet, there are improvised stairs to help with the elevation gain. This section gains about 70 feet, but it doesn't feel like much if you are slowly exploring.

Reach a small grove of aspens in about 550 feet. Watch for wildflowers here in the spring—a botanist's dream. There are a variety of native and endemic blooms, including the endangered Carson monkeyflower, a striking yellow flower marked with a red heart-shaped dot on the bottom petals. Though it may ellude trail users (it is a rare sighting), its mystery and ephemeral presence add a special feeling here. Plus, as you slowly search for it, you will be rewarded with other beautiful blooms of many colors, shapes, and sizes.

At 0.2 mile, come to a creek crossing with an adjacent bench. Across the water, meet back up with the main trail and turn right (east) to begin the climb to the gazebo. About 120 feet after the trails merge, they split again. Both sides, again, are part of this loop. To take the gentlest path to the top, choose the trail on the left that heads east. From here, the way opens up, a striking difference to the creekside section. Appreciate the beautiful rock formations marked with reds, oranges, and pinks on the hills surrounding the trail.

The trail switches back to head southwest at 0.4 mile. Another trail continues straight (east) from this point (see Go Farther). Continue around the bend of the switchback to stay on route to the gazebo. When the trail heads southwest, notice the gazebo—and the remaining ascent, about 110 feet in 0.3 mile. Take breaks, searching for hidden wildflowers or enjoying incoming views of the lake.

The way back to the trailhead on Deadman's Creek Trail rewards hikers with amazing views of Washoe Lake and Mount Rose.

MOUNT ROSE VS. MOUNT ROSE

Talking about Mount Rose can be confusing because it is the name for both the Tahoe basin's third-highest peak (at 10,785 feet) and the adjacent ski resort loved by Renoites. The resort, Mt. Rose–Ski Tahoe, is actually located on Slide Mountain, which gets its name from the sheer south side of the mountain that leads to slides. They don't normally cause much damage, but the 1983 slide on the mountain shed debris along Ophir Creek, damaging homes and farmland, stopping traffic on US Highway 395, and even killed one person.

Mount Rose, the mountain not the resort, is the namesake for adjacent wilderness that extends to Hunter Creek Falls (Trail 20). If the ski runs or height of the mountains don't make an obvious landmark for distinction, Mount Rose's ridgeline should be the key to identification. It gives way to lore; some believe that the mountain looks like the profile of a woman with her hair flowing behind her. But the story goes back before that. The Washoe people said that the woman went looking for her husband and never left the mountain, a tear may even be found along her eye as the snow melts.

Both Slide Mountain and Mount Rose make impressive landmarks across the western horizon and can be seen from almost every hike in this book. However, no other hike gives such a great view to Slide Mountain as Ophir Creek.

At the gazebo, about 0.7 mile into the hike, red rocks line the hilltop. Soak up the view of Washoe Lake and the Sierra ridgeline. Closer to dusk, mule deer might graze here, or a rabbit may scurry from bush to bush. The wind will surely make itself known here, especially during spring and summer. (See the "Washoe Zephyr" sidebar in Trail 39.)

To head back, take the trail to the left (north) that heads northeast. It switchbacks about nine times from the gazebo to the trail intersection and, unfortunately, people have cut the switchbacks. Especially in this environment, with delicate and rare plants, this is not okay. Stay on the main path, following the trail markers that point toward the right direction.

At 0.8 mile is one of these social trails, splitting off to the left (north) down the hill. Keep right along the more obvious trail that loses elevation gradually. In another 300 feet, reach another social trail to the left; again, stay right. Within these switchbacks, the environment almost mirrors that of the creekside side loop as early springtime water trickles down the hillside.

At 1 mile, the trail returns to the junction. Turn left to head westward. When the trail splits in 120 feet, continue straight. This last leg gives a beautiful view of the lake, punctuated with colorful aspens and cottonwoods. Continue the last 0.2 mile back to the trailhead.

GO FARTHER

As you descend from the peak, take a right at the first junction to head east. Here, retrace your steps from earlier in the hike for 0.1 mile, then continue straight east instead of turning right (which would lead back to the summit). This connects to an OHV route (the Washoe Lake to Virginia City trail) that eventually climbs its way into the historical gold mining town.

In about 0.3 mile and 160 feet of elevation gain, the trail merges into the Washoe Lake to Virginia City multi-use trail (see full map at Nevada Off-Highway Vehicles Program website). From here, keep straight (east) to make a 1.2 mile-loop back to the Deadman's Creek trailhead, losing 340 feet of elevation. Or head right (south) to hike another 3.2 miles (with 1260 feet of elevation gain) to the Eagle Valley Viewpoint, which looks over Carson City and puts the majesty of this area into perspective.

ACKNOWLEDGMENTS

The knowledgeable folks at Truckee Meadows Trails, Biggest Little Trails Stewardship, and Tahoe-Pyramid Trail were an immense help in creating the most complete and accurate guide I could for this area. These organizations have been working toward connecting the community to the outdoors, often as volunteers. Without their efforts, the trail systems in our community would be lacking, if not nonexistent. I would also like to thank Christina Thayer, the Washoe County Trails Program Coordinator, for her help and support of local trails. The hard work of these organizations is continuing before our eyes and gives me great hope for the future of our community.

I cannot overstate the emotional support of my partner, Ryan Primeaux. While the above organizations wrangle the wild open lands, Ryan has reeled in the sprinting fears of my imagination and stress. I love you!

If it were not for my dog, Lady, whose relentless pining for the outdoors pushed me outside on my worst days, I don't know that I would have fallen so deeply in love with trails. She knew the therapy of the outdoors before I did. I am grateful for her boundless energy and eagerness to never stop walking into the unknown.

Opposite: *Black willows serve as an oasis along Evans Creek (Trails 15 and 16).*

RESOURCES

LAND MANAGERS

Biggest Little Trail Stewardship
6800 South McCarran Blvd., Reno, NV 89509
www.bltsnv.org
poedunknv@gmail.com

Bureau of Land Management, Sierra Front Field Office
(775) 885-6000
ccfoweb@blm.gov
Washoe County Firearms Discharge Restrictions
Map www.blm.gov/sites/default/files/documents/files/NV-Washoe-County-Firearms-Discharge-Restrictions-Map.pdf

Caughlin Ranch HOA
1070 Caughlin Crossing, Reno NV 89519
(775) 746-1499
www.caughlinhoa.com

City of Reno
(775) 334-2417
General parks and recreation information: (775)334-2262
www.reno.gov/government/departments/
parks-recreation-community-services/parks-trails
Adaptive bike center: (775) 333-7765
Paradise Park Community Garden: (775) 356-3176 or (775) 334-2270

City of Sparks, Parks and Recreation
(775) 353-2376
www.cityofsparks.us/rec_home

Damonte Ranch HOA
(775) 334-7411
info@associasn.com
https://damonteranch.com/home-owners

Nevada Department of Wildlife (NDOW)
(775) 334-3808
wildlife-ed@ndow.state.nv.us
www.ndow.org
Fishing licenses
www.ndow.org/apply-buy/fishing-licenses

Nevada Off-Highway Vehicles Program
(775) 684-2794
ohvinfo@ohv.nv.gov
https://ohv.nv.gov/trails

Nevada State Parks
901 S. Stewart Street, 5th Floor, Suite 5005, Carson City, NV 89701
(775) 684-2770
https://parks.nv.gov

Steamboat Canal and Irrigation Company
(775) 853-1399

State of Nevada Division of Wildlife
(775) 688-1500
US Forest Service
Humboldt-Toiyabe National Forest, Carson Ranger District
Carson District: (775) 882-2766
General, www.fs.usda.gov/htnf
Carson District, www.fs.usda.gov/detail/htnf/about-forest/districts/?cid=fseprd753479

Verdi Library
(775) 345-8104
https://washoecountylibrary.us/libraries/verdi.php

Washoe County Regional Parks and Open Space
(775) 823-6501
www.washoecounty.gov/parks

Washoe Lake State Park (Nevada State Parks)
(775) 687-4319
wlsp@parks.nv.gov
https://parks.nv.gov/parks/washoe-lake

LOCAL ORGANIZATIONS

ArTrail
https://artrail.washoecounty.us/

Biggest Little Trail Stewardship
poedunknv@gmail.com
www.bltsnv.org

City of Reno Micromobility Map
www.reno.gov/community/sustainability/bicycling-around-reno

Friends of Nevada Wilderness
PO Box 9754, Reno, NV 89507
(775) 324-7667
www.nevadawilderness.org

Galena Creek Visitor Center
18250 Mt. Rose Hwy., Reno, NV 89511
(775) 849-4948
visitorcenter@thegreatbasininstitute.org
www.galenacreekvisitorcenter.org

Great Basin Science Sample and Records Library, Nevada Bureau of Mines and Geology
2175 Raggio Parkway, Reno, NV 89512
(775) 682-8766
https://nbmg.unr.edu/GBSSRL

Keep Truckee Meadows Beautiful (KTMB)
Mailing Address: PO Box 7412, Reno, NV, 89510
Office Address: 2601 Plumas St., Reno, NV, 89509
(775) 851-5185
staff@ktmb.org
www.ktmb.org/

Lahontan Audubon Society
PO Box 2304, Reno, NV 89505-2304
contact@nevadaaudubon.org
www.nevadaaudubon.org

Leave No Trace (LNT)
https://lnt.org/why/7-principles

Little Free Library Map
https://app.littlefreelibrary.org/ourmap

Rattlesnake Training for Dogs
https://getrattled.org

Reno-Sparks Indian Colony
www.rsic.org/

RTC Bike Map & Information
https://rtcwashoe.com/public-transportation/cycling

RTC Bus Routes
https://rtcwashoe.com/public-transportation/maps-schedules

Tahoe-Pyramid Trail
4790 Caughlin Parkway, #138
Reno, NV 89519
(775) 825-9868
https://tahoepyramidtrail.org

Teglia's Paradise Park Activity Center
(775) 356-3176
www.reno.gov/government/departments/parks-and-recreation/paradise-park-activity-center

Truckee Meadows Parks Foundation (TMPF)
50 Cowan Drive, Reno, NV 89509
(775) 410-1702
info@tmparksfoundation.org
www.tmparksfoundation.org

Visit Reno Tahoe
www.visitrenotahoe.com/

Washoe County "Truckee Meadow Trails" guide
www.washoecounty.gov/parks/files/TrailsGuideFinal.pdf

Washoe Tribe of NV and CA
919 US Highway 395 North, Gardnerville, NV 89410
(775) 265-8600

INDEX

ABOUT THE AUTHOR

RYAN PRIMEAUX

Helena Guglielmino (pronounced in bad English as *GHOUL-you-MEAN-o*) is a Reno-based writer, hiker, backpacker, and explorer of anywhere her nine-year-old lab mix leads her. An adamant believer that Nevada is not a drive-by state or "full of nothing but dirt" as she often hears, she is committed to seeing it all and sharing it with others to inspire wonder in this overlooked place. Her stories on the environment, adventure, and culture have been published by Roadtrippers, Rails-to-Trails Conservancy, *Reno News & Review*, Outdoors Unlimited, and more.

When not writing—but most especially while writing—she enjoys basking in the fantasies of unturned stones and far-off lands. Follow along at storiesbyhelena.com.

MOUNTAINEERS BOOKS

SKIPSTONE BRAIDED RIVER

recreation • lifestyle • conservation

MOUNTAINEERS BOOKS, including its two imprints, Skipstone and Braided River, is a leading publisher of quality outdoor recreation, sustainability, and conservation titles. As a 501(c)(3) nonprofit, we are committed to supporting the environmental and educational goals of our organization by providing expert information on human-powered adventure, sustainable practices at home and on the trail, and preservation of wilderness.

Our publications are made possible through the generosity of donors, and through sales of 700 titles on outdoor recreation, sustainable lifestyle, and conservation. To donate, purchase books, or learn more, visit us online:

MOUNTAINEERS BOOKS

1001 SW Klickitat Way, Suite 201 • Seattle, WA 98134

800-553-4453 • mbooks@mountaineersbooks.org

www.mountaineersbooks.org

An independent nonprofit publisher since 1960

YOU MAY ALSO LIKE:

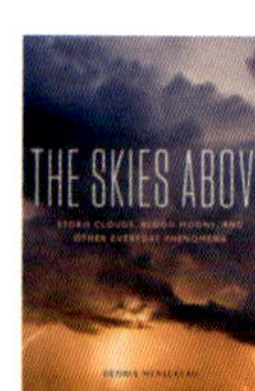

Mountaineers Books is proud to support the Leave No Trace Center for Outdoor Ethics, whose mission is to use the power of science, education, and stewardship to ensure a sustainable future for the outdoors and the planet. The Leave No Trace program is focused specifically on human-powered (nonmotorized) recreation. For more information, visit www.lnt.org.